T0129067

Praise for
Prayers and Promises for Worried Parents

"Most Christians have a family member who is or was a prodigal. By skillfully using pertinent Bible verses and relating remarkable answers to the prayers and faith of parents with prodigals, Rob's book offers hope and comfort to readers. I heartily recommend *Prayers and Promises for Worried Parents*. You will be blessed!"

—M. A. (Joe) Henderson,
executive director emeritus of The Gideons International

"One person has described praying as the most neglected work of the Church. Robert Morgan has provided examples of the historical impact of prayers in the lives of believers and the promises that are ours in the Scriptures accessed through prayer. It seems that our children can send us to our knees quickly and keep us there for a long time. *Prayers and Promises for Worried Parents* is a timely help for burdened parents."

—James Flanagan, Ph.D.,
president of Luther Rice University and Seminary

"In *Prayers and Promises for Worried Parents*, Robert Morgan writes from his own experiences. This book is a great help for parents who are desperate for answers! The book encouraged me to express my heart to God specifically and in detail. My prayer life has been blessed and strengthened as a result."

—Reese R. Kauffman,
president of Child Evangelism Fellowship, Inc.

"Practical. Powerful. Perceptive. Personal. Prayerful. Rob Morgan has crafted a wonderful handbook for all of us with children or friends who are looking for answers in 'all the wrong places.' He teaches all of us that our God listens with great interest to our prayers and gives courage to those who diligently seek Him. Rob carefully takes each of us to the place where prayer and scripture intersect and shows us how to find healing, rest, hope, comfort, and joy, even in the midst of deep and passionate struggle. A must-read for every parent."

—Dr. Vernon M. Whaley,
dean of Liberty University School of Music

Prayers and Promises
for Worried Parents

HOPE FOR YOUR PRODIGAL • HELP FOR YOU

ROBERT J. MORGAN

HOWARD BOOKS
A DIVISION OF SIMON & SCHUSTER, INC.
NEW YORK   NASHVILLE   LONDON   TORONTO   SYDNEY   NEW DELHI

Howard Books
A Division of Simon & Schuster, Inc.
1230 Avenue of the Americas
New York, NY 10020

Copyright © 2003 by Rob Morgan

Originally published as *Moments for Families With Prodigals* in 2003 by NavPress.

All rights reserved, including the right to reproduce this book or portions thereof in any form whatsoever. For information address Howard Books Subsidiary Rights Department, 1230 Avenue of the Americas, New York, NY 10020.

First Howard Books trade paperback edition September 2013

HOWARD and colophon are trademarks of Simon & Schuster, Inc.

For information about special discounts for bulk purchases, please contact Simon & Schuster Special Sales at 1-866-506-1949 or business@simonandschuster.com.

The Simon & Schuster Speakers Bureau can bring authors to your live event. For more information or to book an event, contact the Simon & Schuster Speakers Bureau at 1-866-248-3049 or visit our website at www.simonspeakers.com.

Designed by Davina Mock-Maniscalco

Manufactured in the United States of America

10 9 8 7 6 5 4 3 2 1

Library of Congress Cataloging-in-Publication Data

Morgan, Robert J., 1952–
 [Moments for families with prodigals]
 Prayers and promises for worried parents : hope for your prodigal , help for you / Robert J. Morgan.
  pages cm
 Originally published under title: Moments for families with prodigals : Colorado Springs, Colo. : NavPress, c2003.
 1. Parents—Prayers and devotions. 2. Ex-church members—Family relationships. 3. Meditations. I. Title.
 BV4845.M67 2013
 242'.645—dc23
                         2013010178
ISBN 978-1-4767-4067-6
ISBN 978-1-4767-4068-3 (ebook)

Unless otherwise identified, all Scripture quotations in this publication are taken from the *New King James Version* (NKJV) Copyright © 1982 by Thomas Nelson, Inc. Used by permission. All rights reserved. Other versions used include: the *New American Standard Bible* (NASB) © The Lockman Foundation 1960, 1962, 1963, 1968, 1971, 1972, 1973, 1975, 1977; The HOLY BIBLE: NEW INTERNATIONAL VERSION © (NIV©). Copyright © 1973, 1978, 1984 by International Bible Society used by permission of Zondervan Publishing House, all rights reserved; *The Message: New Testament with Psalms and Proverbs* (MSG) by Eugene H. Peterson. Copyright © 1993, 1994, 1995, used by permission of NavPress Publishing Group; the *Revised Standard Version Bible* (RSV), copyright 1946, 1952, 1971, by the Division of Christian Education of the National Council of the Churches of Christ in the USA, used by permission, all rights reserved; *The New Testament in Modern English* (PH), J. B. Phillips Translator, © J. B. Phillips 1958, 1960, 1972, used by permission of Macmillan Publishing Company; the *New Revised Standard Version* (NRSV), copyright © 1989, by the Division of Christian Education of the National Council of the Churches of Christ in the USA, used by permission, all rights reserved; *The Holy Bible New Century Version* (NCV) copyright © 1987, 1988, 1991 by Word Publishing, Dallas, Texas 75039. Used by permission; the *Good News Bible Today's English Version* (TEV), copyright ‡ American Bible Society 1966, 1975, 1976; the *Amplified New Testament* (AMP), © The Lockman Foundation 1954, 1958; the *Modern Language Bible: The Berkeley Version in Modern English* (MLB), copyright ‡ 1945, 1959, 1969 by Zondervan Publishing House, used by permission; the *Williams New Testament* (WMS) by Charles B. Williams, ‡1937, 1963, 1966, by Edith S. Williams, Moody Bible Institute of Chicago; the *Holy Bible New Living Translation*, (NLT) copyright © 1996. Used by permission of Tyndale House Publishers. Inc., Wheaton, Illinois 60189. All rights reserved.

To Jeff Nichols
My friend and colleague of twenty years.
We have wandered into several valleys together
and always found the way out
. . . with help from above.

Before I was married I had three theories about raising children.
Now I have three children and no theories.

—John Wilmot, Earl of Rochester

Praise ye the Father! For His loving kindness,
Tenderly cares He for His erring children.

—Elizabeth R. Charles, 1858

Contents

Contents

TRUSTING

WEEPING

WAITING

Contents

LEANING

LEARNING

HEALING

Contents

RESTING

HOPING

STRIVING

Contents

SINGING

Foreword

A dear, sweet friend of mine has had nothing but trouble with his children. In my estimation, he has been the perfect parent who provided them with everything they needed to grow up and do the right thing, but every one of them, in one way or another, took a wrong turn. He grieved over them and disciplined them and set proper boundaries with them. After years of cleaning up after their messes and making the best of the worst of situations, some of his prodigal kids came home and some of them did not. From all appearances, his heart was broken over these prodigal kids. But, through it all, his love for them did not falter. To all of us who know him, he is a great example of how to deal with our children when they go the way of the world. He wrote a book about his experiences and it has become a bestseller. My sweet friend is Jesus and, of course, His book is the Bible.

I tell you this to assure you that God is aware of your pain and your struggle. He is not distant from your heart or disinterested in your pain. He has been where you are and is experiencing what you are experiencing right now. You may feel alone in this, but you are not. He wants to guide you and comfort you through every impossible situation and miserable confrontation with your child. And, when you feel like throwing in the towel on parenthood, he wants to give you new strength to carry on the task of loving when it hurts the most.

Over the years I have worked with many parents with children who have ventured out into the religion of *prodigalism*. Their appetites became their gods and the only boundary they set was anything that was possible within the universe. I was with them when they took them to treatment, brought them home afterward, then sometimes watched them go back out again and try to prove that, this time they can handle it. All the while, I ached with them over the total disregard for their love and care. In each instance, I have urged them to do what I want to ask you to do now. It is simply this: grieve the loss of the child you thought you had and begin to love the one you actually have. You simply must move beyond what was and what might have been and move onto what is and what is to be for this lost, confused, broken, and bruised child of yours. It is the best hope for you to keep your sanity and for your child to regain his.

These devotionals are going to help you to do that. They are going to help you grieve and they are going to provide comfort for you as you do. They will help you see your situation from God's perspective, and encourage you to make good decisions, as tough as they may be. They are not intended to be a replacement for treatment for you or your child. Wise counsel and support from strong friends are needed in this battle for your child's soul and your peace of mind. However, this devotional will be a great companion for you as you take time to set your heart straight before you once again try to straighten out your child.

One of my favorite paintings is of a child. It is by Rembrandt and it is of the prodigal son. I love the painting because I see myself in it. Long before I started my ministry I was as lost as any prodigal. So, I connect with the son in the arms of a loving father who took him back home. When you look at that painting, you will notice the hands of the father on the back of the prodigal boy. The hands are very different because, for one, Rembrandt used a female model and for the other he used a male. The soft hand of the female represents God's tender mercy and forgiveness. The strong hand represents the tough love that must be there for every prodigal. Strength and grace—the perfect combination to parent a prodigal.

My prayer for you is that these devotionals will help you grow in both strength and grace, and that they lead you back to the loving arms of your Father. I hope that they will prepare your heart for that time when your child returns to you, or for life if that time never comes. I know the pain and confusion is almost more than you can bear some days, but don't give up on your child. I assure you, God has not. And God has not given up on you. May you find His rich blessings for each new day.

Stephen Arterburn
Founder, New Life Ministries

Preface

Some time ago, while feeling in low spirits over a struggling child, I spoke with a woman in Philadelphia at a seminar I was conducting. She seemed radiant and cheerful, but her smile faded as she told me of her own son, far from the Lord, who had broken her heart. "I prayed for him a long time," she said, "then I sort of ran out of prayers."

At the same seminar, another woman told me of a daughter who had become deeply ensnared in demonism, witchcraft, and the occult. "When she came back to the Lord," said the woman, "she credited my prayers and those of my friends. 'I didn't have a chance against your prayers, Mom,' she told me."

I thought of Jesus' words in Luke 18:1, that we "always ought to pray and not lose heart," and resolved that as long as I lived I would pray for prodigals and, as long I had a Bible, I would never run out of prayers for my children and those of others.

Here is my own collection of prayers, promises, and insights, which helped me during a painful period of life. I hope they'll encourage you, too. If so, please contact me through my website at www.robertjmorgan.com.

We should, after all, never give up. Prodigals have a way of coming home.

Throughout this book I've used the masculine gender to avoid the awkward he/she format, and because the majority of prodigals are males.¹ My original prayers used "she" and "they," because I have daughters and no sons. I'm so glad for our renewed relationship today. They've given me permission to use pieces of their stories, as I retell my anguish that led to times of extended prayer. Please insert your own child's name as you pray along with me.

1

The Power of Praying-a-Phrase of Scripture

Several years ago, my wife Katrina and I took in a troubled young man with a long history of drug and alcohol abuse. We loved him dearly. After six months of apparent progress, he relapsed. We'll call him Mark.

The next months felt like a nightmare, but Mark finally consented to let us enroll him in a drug rehabilitation program. He entered just before his birthday. I told him that instead of giving him a present, on his birthday I would pray for him for an hour.

When the day came, I wondered how I could pray so long for one person. I waited until everyone had gone to bed, and I knelt by the living room sofa with an open Bible before me. I started in Genesis and thumbed through page after page. Before me lay well-worn chapters, underlined verses, and highlighted passages. One by one I converted them into prayers for Mark. Seldom have I felt such power in prayer, and the hour went quickly. I ran out of time long before running out of verses.

Meanwhile, in the rehab center, Mark turned the corner.

If, in dealing with your children's problems, you find your stomach knotting, your head pounding, and your teeth clenched, discover the simple remedy of bending your knees. Plead the promises of God and learn to pray-a-phrase of Scripture. In other words, find some verses that you would like to pray and put your child's name in them.[2]

Throughout this devotional, you'll find many prayers adapted from some of the Bible's greatest passages, as well as from ancient prayers of godly saints and the tender prayers of some of our best-loved hymns. Make them personal for your need and soon you'll be praying-a-phrase of Scripture whenever you read the Bible.

2

The Bible's Most Powerful
Prayers for Prodigals

Consider these verses, which are usually significant for loved ones burdened for their prodigals:

Dear Lord,

Please work in _____ , that he might both will and do Your good pleasure. . . . Work in him what is pleasing to You. . . . Give him the desire to do Your will.

Incline _____'s heart to Yourself, to walk in all Your ways.

Bring him to his senses. Deliver him from evil. Draw him to Yourself. Deliver him from every evil work and preserve him for Your heavenly kingdom.

Bring him out of the miry clay, set his feet upon a rock, and establish his steps. Put a new song in his mouth, even of praise to You.

I do not pray that You would take _____ out of the world, but that You would keep him from the evil one. Sanctify him by Your truth.

*Create in him a clean heart, O God, and renew a
steadfast spirit within him.*

*Most High, establish him. You have begun a good work
in him; now carry it on to completion. Perfect that which
concerns him. May he stand firm in all Your will, mature
and fully assured.*

(Adapted from Philippians 2:13; Hebrews 13:21; 1 Kings 8:58;
Luke 15:17; Matthew 6:13; John 6:44; 2 Timothy 4:10;
Psalm 40:1–3; John 17:15, 17; Psalm 51:10, 87:5;
Philippians 1:6; Psalm 138:8; Colossians 4:12.)

3

What God Can Do

N ever stop praying for so-called hopeless cases. The example of E. Howard Cadle teaches us there are none.

Cadle grew up in the home of a Christian mother and an alcoholic father. By age twelve, he began to emulate his father, drinking and raging out of control. Soon, he succumbed to the power of sex, gambling, and the Midwest crime syndicate.

"Always remember, son," his worried mother often said, "that at eight o'clock every night I'll be kneeling beside your bed, asking God to protect my precious boy." Her prayers didn't seem to slow him down until one evening, on a rampage, he pulled a gun on a man and squeezed the trigger. The weapon never fired, and someone quickly knocked it away. Cadle noticed it was exactly eight o'clock.

Later, in broken health, he was told by a doctor that he had only six months to live. Dragging himself home, penniless and pitiful, he collapsed in his mother's arms, saying, "Mother, I've broken your heart. I'd like to be saved, but I've sinned too much."

The old woman opened her Bible and read Isaiah 1:18: "Though your sins are like scarlet, they shall be as white as snow." That windswept morning, March 14, 1914, Cadle started life anew. With Christ now in his heart, he turned his con skills into honest pursuits and started making money hand over fist, giving 75 percent of it to the Lord's work. He helped finance Rodney "Gipsy" Smith's crusades, in which thousands came to faith in Christ. Then, he began preaching on Cincinnati's powerful WLW, becoming one of America's most popular radio evangelists. "Until He calls me," Cadle used to say, "I shall preach the same gospel that caused my sainted mother to pray for me. And when I have gone to the last city and preached my last sermon, I want to sit at His feet and say, 'Thank You, Jesus, for saving me that dark and stormy day from a drunkard's and a gambler's Hell.'"[3]

While we're to pray without ceasing—and many of us find ourselves praying day and night for our children—it does help to have specific, disciplined habits of prayer on behalf of a wayward child. You might find a prayer partner who will covenant to pray with you at the same time each week. Prayer will win the victory, and the faithful prayers of a parent or grandparent are among the most potent forces in the universe.

4

The Kneeling Christian

I found myself far from home, in Florida, trying to minister to others when my own spirits had begun to falter. On the side shelf of a dusty bookstore, I found what I needed: an old, worn copy of *The Kneeling Christian,* marked at $1.50. I would have paid ten times that price. The owner glanced at the book, shrugged, and said, "You can have it for seventy-five cents."

The months that followed were tremendously stressful. *The Kneeling Christian* became my constant comfort and friend. I consider it the greatest classic on prayer in my library.

We know little about the background of this book because its author, Albert Ernest Richardson, didn't want us to know his name. He wrote several books under the pseudonym "An Unknown Christian." I uncovered his name with the help of my friend Chuck Sherrill and his contacts at the British Library. Over the years, *The Kneeling Christian* has been reprinted in many languages by many publishing houses. The twelve short chapters deal with such subjects as:

- God's Great Need

- Almost Incredible Promises

- How Shall I Pray?

- Must I Agonize?

- Does God Always Answer Prayer?

I include several excerpts from *The Kneeling Christian* in this book, especially Richardson's observation about the Upper Room passages of John 13–16, in which he noted that Jesus invites us seven times to ask for *anything* in His name. The Master spoke just before His arrest; within twenty-four hours His cold body would rest in the tomb. He had precious little time to prepare His disciples in that upper room, yet seven times He promised them that God would answer their prayers. Richardson wrote:

> *Six times over, almost in the same breath, our Savior commands us to ask whatsoever we will. This is the greatest—the most wonderful—promise ever made. Yet most practically ignore it. We have often spent time in reflecting on our Lord's seven words from the cross, [but] have we ever spent one hour in meditating upon our Savior's sevenfold invitation to pray?*[4]

After reading those words, I scoured John 13–16 and listed these seven promises of Jesus in my prayer journal. They belong to you as well.

1. I will do whatever you ask in my name, so that the Son may bring glory to the Father.

    —John 14:13 (NIV)

2. You may ask me for anything in my name, and I will do it.

    —14:14 (NIV)

3. If you remain in me and my words remain in you, ask whatever you wish, and it will be given you

—15:7 (NIV)

4. You did not choose me, but I chose you and appointed you to go and bear fruit—fruit that will last. Then the Father will give you whatever you ask in my name.

—15:16 (NIV)

5. In that day you will no longer ask me anything. I tell you the truth, my Father will give you whatever you ask in my name.

—16:23 (NIV)

6. Until now you have not asked for anything in my name. Ask and you will receive, and your joy will be complete.

—16:24 (NIV)

7. In that day you will ask in my name.... The Father himself loves you.

16:26–27 (NIV)

Underline these words in your Bible and remind the Lord of them. He doesn't mind being reminded of His promises, for He has every intention of keeping them.

5

A Prayer from Proverbs

Today, focus on your desire to see your child live a godly life:

Lord, please grant _____
The good sense to choose friends carefully.
The wisdom to act prudently.
Godly fear.
A wholesome tongue.
Slowness to anger.
Diligence and industriousness.
Honesty.
Direction in his steps.
Wariness of alcohol.
Purity of heart.
A tender conscience.
Wise counsel from others.
An excellent life partner.

(Adapted from Proverbs 12:26; 13:16; 14:26; 15:4, 18;
10:4–5; 11:1; 16:9; 20:1; 22:11; 20:27; 24:6; 12:4.)

6

Thomas Watson on Prayer

T homas Watson, a Puritan preacher in seventeenth-century England, had a powerful pulpit ministry, a very readable writing style, and a gift of prayer. His writings are among the most enjoyable of those of the Puritans and, during my most depressing moments, his messages encouraged me. He died in his prayer closet while interceding before God's throne. Consider some of his thoughts on prayer, compiled from his various books and sermons.

> *Prayer delights God's ear, it melts His heart, it opens His hand: God cannot deny a praying soul.*

> *It is one thing to pray, another thing to be given to prayer: he who prays frequently is said to be given to prayer; as he who often distributes alms, is said to be given to charity.*

> *To pray in the name of Christ is not only to mention Christ's name in prayer, but to pray in the hope and confidence of his merits. "Samuel took a lamb and offered it . . ." (1 Samuel*

7:9). We must carry the lamb Christ in the arms of our faith, and so shall we prevail in prayer.

When Uzziah would offer incense without a priest, God was angry and struck him with leprosy (2 Chronicles 26:16). When we do not pray in Christ's name, in the hope of His mediation, we offer up incense without a priest.

Faith is to prayer what the feather is to the arrow; it feathers the arrow of prayer, and makes it fly swifter, and pierce the throne of grace.[5]

7

Praying for a Life Wholly His

Today, focus on your desire to see your child's life belong to God alone:

I beseech You, O Lord, in view of Your mercies, bowing and
begging and baring my soul, to work in my child, making
him whole, and making him wholly Yours.

I ask that his body would be all Your own, Your home,
dear Lord, Your royal throne, holy and happy and hallowed
for You, a life that is wholly Yours.

I pray that the world would lose its appeal, its seducing
allure. May he not be conformed to its pleasures and patterns
and parties and thrills.

But transformed from above, established by grace,
and fulfilling Your holy will.

(Adapted from Romans 12:1–2.)

8

John "Praying" Hyde's Remarkable Verses

One day, I became very intrigued by Isaiah 62:6–7, a passage that literally tells us to give God no rest until He grants our requests.

> *I have set watchmen on your walls, O Jerusalem;*
> *They shall never hold their peace day or night.*
> *You who make mention of the LORD, do not keep silent,*
> *And give Him no rest till He establishes*
> *And till He makes Jerusalem a praise in the earth.*

One translation of this passage says, "They must remind the Lord of his promises. . . . They must give him no rest until He restores Jerusalem." In other words, we should remind God of His promises and give Him no rest until He answers.

This passage taught John "Praying" Hyde to intercede for others with power and persistence. Hyde grew up in Carthage, Illinois, in a minister's home. At McCormick Theological Seminary, he committed himself to overseas evangelism and, after graduation, left for India. His itinerant ministry took him from village to village, but his preaching produced few converts until he discovered the truth of Isaiah 62:6–7, and took those words literally.

At the beginning of 1908, he prayed to win at least one soul to Christ every day. By December 31, he had recorded over four hundred converts. The following year, the Lord laid two souls per day on his heart, and his prayer again was answered. The next year he prayed for four souls daily, with similar results.

Once, stopping at a cottage for water, Praying Hyde pleaded with God for ten souls. He presented the gospel to the family, and by the end of his visit all nine family members had come to faith. What of number ten? Suddenly, a nephew who had been playing outside ran into the room and ended up trusting Christ for salvation.

Ruth Bell Graham once told me, "God loves to be reminded of His promises. He never rebukes us for asking too much."

In his book, *Prevailing Prayer,* evangelist D. L. Moody wrote, "So if you are anxious about the conversion of some relative, or some friend, make up your mind that you will give God no rest, day or night, till He grants your petition. He can reach them, wherever they are—at their places of business, in their homes, or anywhere—and bring them to His feet."[6]

This same passage in Isaiah is an exhortation for each of us:

You people who remind the Lord of your needs in prayer should never be quiet. You should not stop praying to Him. Take no rest, all you who pray. Give the Lord no rest. . . . Remind Him of His promises, and never let Him forget them.

(Adapted from Isaiah 62:6–7.)

9

Prayer to Be Reckoned With

During my years of inward struggle, I adopted James 5:16 as my favorite verse on prayer. It is a demanding verse, for it implies that the effective prayer warrior must keep his or her life clean. Notice the key adjective describing the praying person: *righteous*. Ultimately, we become righteous only in Christ, but the righteousness of Christ should show up in our lives in practical ways, among those, faithfulness in prayer. Read this verse in several translations:

> *The effective, fervent prayer of a righteous man avails much.*

> *The prayer of a righteous man is powerful and effective.* (NIV)

> *The earnest prayer of a righteous person has great power and wonderful results.* (NLT)

> *The earnest (heartfelt, continued) prayer of a righteous man makes tremendous power available.* (AMP)

> *When a believing person prays, great things happen.* (NCV)

16

The prayer of a person living right with God is something powerful to be reckoned with. (MSG)

An upright man's prayer, when it keeps at work, is very powerful. (WMS)

Tremendous power is made available through a good man's earnest prayer. (PH)

10

Prevailing Prayer

C onsider these quotes on the importance of prevailing prayer:

> *Is it not a fact that the majority of Christian men and women who pray to a living God know very little about real, prevailing prayer? Yet prayer is the key which unlocks the door of God's treasure house. It is not too much to say that all real growth in the spiritual life—all victory over temptation, all confidence and peace in the presence of difficulties and dangers, all repose of spirit during times of great disappointment or loss, all habitual communion with God—depend on the practice of secret prayer.*[7]
>
> —AN UNKNOWN CHRISTIAN

> *Jacob, who in his contest with the Angel of Jehovah had prevailed by prayer and entreaty, now also prevails by humility and modesty against Esau, who comes to meet him with four hundred men.*
>
> —ALFRED EDERSHEIM

If you are enabled to prevail in prayer you will have many requests to offer for others who will flock to you, and beg a share in your intercessions, and so you will find yourselves commissioned with errands to the mercy-seat for friends and hearers.

—Charles H. Spurgeon

It is the prayer of faith that is the prevailing prayer. His faith pleads with God, orders the cause, and fills his mouth with arguments. He acts faith especially upon the righteousness of God, and is very confident.

—Matthew Henry

In our spiritual conflicts, we must look up to heaven for strength; and it is the believing prayer that will be the prevailing prayer.

—Matthew Henry

In prevailing prayer, a child of God comes before Him with real faith in His promises and asks for things agreeable to His will, assured of being heard according to the true intent of the promises; and thus coming to God he prevails with Him.

—Charles Finney

Prevailing prayer is the pathway to the outpouring of the Holy Spirit.

—John Piper

Here's a prevailing prayer adapted from Jeremiah 24:6–7:

Lord,
Please set Your eyes on _____ for good and bring him back to this land. Build him up, and do not pull

him down; plant him, and do not pluck him up. Give him a heart to know You, that You are the Lord. Be his God, and reclaim him as Your humble, obedient, triumphant child. May he return to You with his whole heart.

In Jesus' name. Amen.

11

Command Light to Shine

Today, focus on your desire for your child to see God:

I trust You, Lord. You are the God of all comfort who comforts us in all our tribulation that we may be able to comfort others who are in any trouble.

You know my deep concern for my child. I fear that just as the serpent deceived Eve by his craftiness, he may deceive my child and turn him from the way, corrupting his mind to the simplicity of Christ.

Command light to shine into _____ 's heart to give him the knowledge of the glory of God. Restrain him from linking up with unbelievers. May he come out from among them and be separate. May he cleanse himself from all filthiness of the flesh and spirit, perfecting holiness in Your sight.

Here before Your throne, Lord, the weapons of my warfare are mighty through God for pulling down strongholds. In earnest prayer, I pull down the satanic strongholds that are unsettling my child.

I ask Your all-sufficient grace to give us the victory.

(Adapted from 2 Corinthians.)

12

God's Faithfulness

Today, focus on your desire for your child to recognize God's faithfulness:

O Lord, Your faithfulness reaches to the clouds.
Your faithfulness surrounds You . . . and endures to all
generations. All Your commandments are faithful. . . . Your
testimonies are righteous and very faithful.

By faith Sarah herself received strength to conceive seed,
and she bore a child when she was past the age, because she
judged You faithful and You had promised.

You called us, and You are faithful. Lord, You are
faithful, who will establish us and guard us from the evil one.

Therefore, we know that You the Lord our God are God,
the faithful God who keeps covenant and mercy for a
thousand generations with those who love You and keep Your
commandments.

Faithfulness is the belt of Your waist.

Judah still walks with You, even as You are the Holy
One who is faithful.

If his sons forsake Your law and do not walk in Your judgments . . . then You will punish their transgression with the rod, and their iniquity with stripes. Nevertheless in Your loving kindness You will not utterly take from him, nor allow Your faithfulness to fail.

If we are faithless, You remain faithful.

You are faithful and just to forgive us our sins . . . a merciful and faithful High Priest . . . Jesus Christ, the faithful witness.

Through Your mercies, Lord, we are not consumed, because Your compassions fail not. They are new every morning; great is Your faithfulness.

Now John saw heaven opened, and behold, a white horse. And You who sat on him were called Faithful and True.

Help us hold fast the confession of our hope without wavering, for You promised and You are faithful.

(Adapted from Psalms 36:5, 89:8, 119:90, 86, 138;
Hebrews 11:11; 1 Thessalonians 5:24; 2 Thessalonians 3:3;
Deuteronomy 7:9; Isaiah 11:5; Hosea 11:12; Psalm 89:30–33;
2 Timothy 2:13; 1 John 1:9; Hebrews 2:17; Revelation 1:5;
Lamentations 3:22–23; Revelation 19:11; Hebrews 10:23.)

13

A Shaft of Light on a Dismal Day

Nothing encourages troubled parents more than the support of other parents who have lived long enough to see their anguished prayers for their own children answered. My friend, Dr. Bob Hill, told me the following story, which I've included with his and his son's permission. It hit me like a shaft of light on an otherwise dismal day.

> *During his senior year of high school, things went downhill with our son, Rob. He began hanging around with friends we didn't approve of. He told us they went to church, but we knew they weren't good for him.*
>
> *Rob's first year of college was difficult. He began drinking and partying, got failing grades, and dropped out. Not knowing what else to do, we suggested he join the army, but there he did worse than ever, running with the wrong crowd and drinking heavily.*
>
> *He called home about once a month, but only to ask for money. He never seemed concerned about how we were . . . just wanted money. We finally felt that by giving*

him money we were contributing to his delinquency, so we stopped supporting him.

Then, one night, I had a vivid dream in which he and I were out in a small fishing boat on the river. Suddenly, the boat tipped over, sending us underwater. I swam to shore, but couldn't find Rob. I called and looked everywhere, but he was gone. At the moment of my greatest desperation, I looked down the river about two hundred yards to find he had resurfaced and was sitting on a rock.

"Here I am, Dad!" he called. "I'm all right." Just then, I awoke, and Proverbs 22:6 came strongly to mind: "Train up a child in the way he should go, and when he is old he will not depart from it." I awakened my wife, related my dream, and told her I had a peace that Rob was going to come through this all right.

About two years later, Rob got out of the army, returned home, and made a complete turnaround. He started going to church with us and married a wonderful Christian girl. Now they have three precious children, and he teaches Sunday school and lives for the Lord with all his heart.[8]

"I really believe," Bob added, "that Proverbs 22:6 is God's assurance for parents during times when their children may be drifting."

I have found this verse very comforting. Biblical scholars interpret it in various ways, but for me it's just as Bob said—God's assurance.

Train up a child in the way he should go, and when he is old he will not depart from it. (NIV)

Point your kids in the right direction—when they're old they won't be lost. (MSG)

Teach children how they should live, and they will remember it all their life. (TEV)

Educate a child according to his life requirements; even when he is old he will not veer from it. (MLB)

Teach your children right from wrong, and when they are grown they will still do right. (CEV)

When they have conquered early fears,
and vanquished youthful wrong
Grace will preserve their following years,
and make their virtues strong.
—Author Unknown

14

A Simple Prayer

Today, simply pray for God's power to touch your child in every way:

Lord, I pray for _____ *this simple prayer:*

Pull him from his sins.
Cover him with Your blood.
Protect him by Your angels.
Draw him by Your grace.
Melt him with Your love.
Mold him into Your image.
Fill him with Your Spirit.
Use him for Your glory.

Amen.

15

❧

Saul? Or David?

My child seemed safe and sound last night, but I wasn't sure and I felt scared . . . nervous . . . ill at ease. I fretted all evening, the very thing that the Lord condemns in Psalm 37. I tossed and turned in bed, beset by nameless, nagging worries.

This morning's Bible reading took me to 1 Samuel 17: David and Goliath. Though I knew the story, I'd never seen it quite as I did today. In this passage, Goliath threatened the children of Israel (even as the giants of peer pressure, temptation, and the Devil himself threaten our own children).

However, I saw something new. The real lesson of 1 Samuel 17 is not the comparison between David and Goliath, but between young David and the old, apostate King Saul.

King Saul's reaction appears in verse 11: "When Saul and all Israel heard these words of the Philistine, they were dismayed and greatly afraid." Saul compared himself with the giant, instead of comparing the giant with God. Therefore, he felt worried and anxious. Ill at ease. Fretting. Dismayed and greatly afraid.

Exactly like me.

David's take on the situation appears in verse 47: "The battle is the Lord's." He didn't underestimate the difficulty, but neither did he underestimate his ally: "The Lord, who delivered me from the paw of the lion and from the paw of the bear, He will deliver me from the hand of this Philistine" (verse 37).

Lord, thank You for reminding me that both the battle and the victory are Yours. Forgive my Saul-ishness. May I be more like David in this time. Make me a man after Your own heart—trusting, calm, confident, wise, waiting for Your arm to win the victory.

And show me how to use that spiritual slingshot as needed.

16

A Prayer for Power

Today, focus on your desire to know that God has touched your child:

*Father, I bow my knees to You, the Father of our Lord
Jesus Christ, asking You to grant* _____
*according to the riches of Your glory to be strengthened and
reinforced with mighty power in his inner being by Your
Holy Spirit, that Christ may be at home in his heart
through faith.*

*I pray that my son will become rooted deeply in love and
will be able to comprehend with all the saints that which is
the width and length and depth and height of Your love. And
may he really come to know—practically, through
experience for himself—the love of Christ, which far
surpasses knowledge.*

*Dear Lord, may my child come to have the richest
measure of Your divine presence in his life. May his very
body become wholly filled and flooded with You.*

Now to You who are able, by that power that is at work

within us, to do far above all that I dare ask or think—
beyond my highest prayers, desires, thoughts, hopes, or
dreams—to You be glory throughout all generations, forever
and ever. Amen.

(Adapted from Ephesians 3:14–21.)

17

Leave Room for God

One night, when I was worried sick about my child, I found four words sitting quietly on page 1291 of my Bible. I'd read them many times before but, this time, as I stared at them, they fairly flew at me like stones from a slingshot. The four words, now well underlined, are *Leave room for God*—from the phrase "leave room for God's wrath" (Romans 12:19, niv).

The immediate context involves retribution. When someone harms us, advises the writer, we shouldn't try to get even, but should leave room for God's wrath and let Him settle the score.

And, if we can leave room for God's wrath, then, when facing other challenges, can we not leave room for His other attributes? For His power? For His grace? For His intervention? I underlined the words, "Leave room for God," and have leaned on them ever since.

There are times to get proactive with our prodigal children but, at other times, even our best efforts will not solve the problem or alter the situation. In those cases, we must leave room for God to work, praying and waiting for Him. Cameron V. Thompson wrote:

We must let God work. That is, we should not try to answer our own prayers, unless the Lord Himself should lead that way. Shall we take a sieve and try to make a passage through the Red Sea by bailing out the water, or shall we push at the walls of Jericho while marching around them? "Commit thy way unto [roll thy way upon] the LORD; trust also in Him; and He shall bring it to pass" (Psalm 37:5).[9]

So, leave room for God; He alone can storm the impregnable, devise the improbable, and perform the impossible.

18

Fainting Fits

During my child's prodigal period, I also had to deal with my wife Katrina's debilitating illness, the financial drain we took on by sending our kids to college, and the demands of a growing ministry. At times I wondered if I could bear it all. One day I searched out verses about strength, and that's when I realized I didn't *have* to bear it all. The Lord bears our burdens and imparts His strength. Ponder a medley of verses on this subject.

> *My strength is dried up like a potsherd. My strength fails me. No strength remains in me.*
>
> *We are burdened beyond measure, above strength.*
>
> *You, God, are our refuge and strength, a very present help in trouble. Therefore we will not fear. . . . You, the God of Israel, give strength and power to Your people. Blessed be God! . . . You have been a strength to the poor, a strength to the needy in his distress, a refuge from the storm, a shade from the heat.*
>
> *[You have said,] "Take hold of My strength. I will strengthen you, yes, I will help you. . . . My grace is*

sufficient for you, for My strength is made perfect in weakness."

O Lord, You are my strength and my shield . . . my strength and my song . . . my strength and my fortress . . . my strength and my power. You are my light and my salvation; whom shall I fear? You are the strength of my life; of whom shall I be afraid?

I can do all things through Christ who strengthens me.

(Adapted from Psalms 22:15, 38:10; Daniel 10:8; 2 Corinthians 1:8; Psalms 46:1–2; 68:35; Isaiah 25:4, 27:5, 41:10; 2 Corinthians 12:9; Psalms 28:7; 118:14; Jeremiah 16:19; 2 Samuel 22:33; Psalm 27:1; Philippians 4:13.)

19

John's Prodigal

According to tradition, the aged apostle John once was visiting the churches on his circuit when he spotted a handsome boy of powerful physique, who seemed to have enormous potential. John committed the nurturing of the youth to one of his bishops. Sometime later, again visiting the area, John inquired about the young man. The bishop's face fell.

"Alas," he said, "he is dead. He is dead to God. He has become a prodigal. A dissolute band of troublemakers has drawn him among them, and he has become a bandit."

Hearing this, John tore his clothes and called for a horse. He rode from the church in haste, found the band of outlaws, and confronted the young man. According to tradition, the youth turned to flee, so great was his shame. But the apostle called out, "Why, my son, do you run from me, your own father, unarmed and aged? Pity me, son; fear not. You still have hope of life. If need be, I will die in your place."

The youth returned, and the two men embraced, wept, and knelt in prayer. The prodigal was restored.

Offer the following prayer for your loved one, woven from the words of the apostle John as found in his first epistle.

Father,

We love You because You first loved us. You love
_____ *even more than I do, therefore I know my*
prayer is finding a sympathetic ear. You have promised to
grant whatever I ask if it is according to Your will.

My petition then, Lord, is this: Show my child that all
that is in the world—the lust of the flesh, the lust of the eyes,
and the pride of life—is not from You, but is of the world.
Help him see that the world is passing away, and the lust of
it, but the one who does Your will abides forever.

Teach him to confess his sins. Teach him to purify himself.
Teach him to walk in the light as You are in the light. Teach
him to walk just as Christ walked.

And Lord, teach me not to be afraid, but to trust Your
love, for there is no fear in love. Increase my faith and give
me the victory that has overcome the world. . . .

I pray this in the name of the One who came to destroy
the works of the Devil, . . . in the authority of the One who is
greater than he who is in the world.

(Adapted from 1 John 4:19, 5:14–15,
2:15–17, 1:9, 3:3, 1:7, 2:6, 4:18, 5:4, 3:8, 4:4)

20

⟨⟨⟨⟩⟩⟩

When God Doesn't Seem
to Answer Our Prayers

I had earnestly prayed for my child about a certain matter involving a phone call, then the Lord allowed the exact opposite of what I had requested. I felt bewildered and angry. However, that morning's Bible reading took me to Psalm 18, where verse 30 struck me: "As for God, His way is perfect."

Later that day I came across a wise quote from Ruth Bell Graham: "How often has God said no to my earnest prayers that He might answer my deepest longings, give me something more, something better." Or, as Cameron V. Thompson put it: "As the Lord has made each leaf different, so also He shows limitless variety and divine ingenuity in answering prayer."

Time and time again, the writings of other Christians show that God's way is best:

> But Thou, taking Thy own secret counsel and noting the real
> point of her desire, didst not grant what she was then asking
> in order to grant to her the thing that she had always been
> asking.

So Augustine wrote about his mother, Monica, who prayed earnestly that her son would not sail to Italy, for she feared the bad influences awaiting him there. Despite her prayers, Augustine did go to Italy, and there he found Christ.

When we pray for our children, we are asking God to make His presence a part of their lives and work powerfully in their behalf. That doesn't mean there will always be an immediate response. Sometimes, it can take days, weeks, or even years. But our prayers are never lost or meaningless. If we are praying, something is happening, whether or not we see it.

—STORMIE OMARTIAN

Patience frees the Lord to answer prayer in His way and in His time. God never is in a rush, even though we usually are. Waiting on God allows Him to provide the best answer.

—T. W. HUNT AND CLAUDE KING

God wants us to trust Him, no matter what He does. There is a heavenly carelessness that leaves it all with Jesus and doesn't become upset when He does things contrary to what we expected.

—VANCE HAVNER

21

Tears

Few of us can endure our children's hard times without shedding tears. I recall a night when I had to tell a hard-nosed, successful businessman that his son had relapsed into the murky world of alcoholism and drug abuse. He screamed into the phone, then shouted unanswerable questions, then broke down into wracking sobs.

I know about shedding such tears—and so does God. Searching for what the Bible says about weeping can bring great comfort.

Jesus wept. . . . He groaned in the spirit and was troubled.

—JOHN 11:35, 33

I have heard your prayer, I have seen your tears.

—2 KINGS 20:5

My eyes pour out tears to God.

—JOB 16:20

Put my tears in Your bottle;
Are they not in Your book?
When I cry out to You,
Then my enemies will turn back;
This I know because God is for me.
In God (I will praise His word),
In the LORD (I will praise His word),
In God I have put my trust;
I will not be afraid.
—PSALM 56:8–11

Those who sow in tears
Shall reap in joy.
He who continually goes forth weeping,
Bearing seed for sowing,
Shall doubtless come again with rejoicing,
Bringing his sheaves with him.
—PSALM 126:5–6

Weeping may endure for a night,
But joy comes in the morning.
—Psalm 30:5

Refrain your voice from weeping, and your eyes from tears;
for your work shall be rewarded, says the LORD, and they
shall come back from the land of the enemy. There is hope
in your future, says the LORD, that your children will come
back to their own border.

—JEREMIAH 31:16–17

It is not possible that the son of such tears should be lost.
—FROM AUGUSTINE'S *CONFESSIONS*, SPOKEN TO MONICA
BY HER PASTOR REGARDING HER WAYWARD SON, AUGUSTINE

> *Weeping prayer prevails.*
>
> —THOMAS WATSON,
> SEVENTEENTH-CENTURY PURITAN

Your tears are precious to God. He specializes in hearing tearful prayer and in healing broken hearts.

22

Open His Eyes

The tears in our eyes are sometimes converted, through prayer, into eye drops for our prodigals. As we pray through our tears, the Lord hears our requests and opens our prodigals' eyes. The Bible has much to say about God's ability to open blinded eyes. Take this prayer as your own today.

Lord, open his eyes that he may see.

You open the eyes of the blind and raise those who are bowed down. Now, please give _____ a heart to perceive Your will, eyes to see Your way, and ears to hear Your Word.

This is my ceaseless prayer, that You, the Father of glory, would give to my child the spirit of wisdom and revelation in the knowledge of Christ, the eyes of his heart being enlightened; that he might know the hope of Christ's calling, the riches of Christ's glorious inheritance in the saints, and the exceeding greatness of Christ's power toward those who believe.

Lord, that his eyes may be opened . . . anoint his eyes with

43

Your salve. Open his understanding that he might comprehend Scripture. . . . Open his eyes and turn him from darkness to light, from the power of Satan to You, that he may receive forgiveness of sins and an inheritance among those who are sanctified by faith in You.

Grant him the testimony of him who said, "One thing I know: though I was blind, now I see."

(Adapted from 2 Kings 6:17; Psalm 146:8; Deuteronomy 29:4; Ephesians 1:16–20; Matthew 20:33; Revelation 3:18; Luke 24:45; Acts 26:18; John 9:25.)

23

Lord, Incline . . .

S ometimes a concordance proves very helpful in praying. Once, for example, I looked up all the Bible references with the word *incline*. It's a powerful prayer verb when God is the subject and our child is the direct object.

> *Lord, incline _____ 's heart to Yourself, to walk in all Your ways, and to keep Your commandments and statutes and judgments. Incline his heart to perform Your statutes forever, to the very end.*
>
> *Let not his heart be inclined to any evil thing, to practice wicked works with those who work iniquity. . . . Cause him to put away other gods and to incline his heart toward You, the Lord God of Israel.*
>
> *Incline his ear to wisdom . . . his ears to the words of Your mouth . . . and his heart to Your testimonies, and not to covetousness.*
>
> (Adapted from 1 Kings 8:58; Psalms 119:112, 141:4;
> Joshua 24:23; Proverbs 2:2; Psalms 78:1, 119:36.)

24

Singleness of Heart and Action

Jeremiah was called the weeping prophet because he preached to stubborn people in a degraded age amid war's devastation. Yet I always find strength and courage when reading the words of this old, melancholy prophet. Read Jeremiah 32 for your own blessing, then offer this short, simple prayer for your child, adapted from that chapter.

> *Sovereign Lord,*
>
> *You made the heavens and the earth by Your great power and outstretched arm. Nothing is too hard for You. Now, please give _____ singleness of heart and action, that he will fear You for his own good and the good of his children after him.*
>
> *In Jesus' name. Amen.*

25

Praying for the Mind of Christ

Today, focus on your desire to see your child come to know Christ personally:

Heavenly Father, give _____ *the mind of Christ.*

Help him work out his salvation with fear and trembling, even as You work in him both to will and to do Your good pleasure.

Help him, Father, to become blameless and pure, a child of Yours without fault in this crooked and depraved world, so that I may boast on the day of Christ that I did not run or labor for nothing.

Lord, have mercy upon my child—and upon me, too, to spare me sorrow upon sorrow.

(Adapted from Philippians 2.)

26

Divine Tissues

Consider the following promises and reassurances, which are able to dry your eyes like divine tissues. Read them and choose one to take with you into the day or to keep you through the night.

> *Call to Me, and I will answer you, and show you great and mighty things, which you did not know.*
>
> —JEREMIAH 33:3

> *When you pray, go into your room, and when you have shut your door, pray to your Father who is in the secret place; and your Father who sees in secret will reward you openly.*
>
> —MATTHEW 6:6

> *What human father among you, when his son asks him for bread, will give him a stone? Or if he asks for a fish, will he give him a snake? So if you, in spite of your being bad, know how to give your children what is good, how much more*

*surely will your heavenly Father give what is good to those
who keep on asking Him?*

—Matthew 7:9–11 (wms)

*Now to Him who is able to do exceedingly abundantly
above all that we ask or think, according to the power that
works in us, to Him be glory in the church by Christ Jesus to
all generations, forever and ever. Amen.*

—Ephesians 3:20–21

*Thou art coming to a King
Large petitions with thee bring;
For His grace and power are such
None can ever ask too much.*
—John Newton

27

The Prodigal and God's Providence

Christian parents often worry about sending their sons and daughters to colleges and universities. Sometimes, with good reason. Young people can lose their faith there; some lose it only to regain it later, with added strength.

Adoniram Judson grew up in parsonages around Boston in the 1700s. He entered Brown University at age sixteen and graduated valedictorian of his class. While there, he became best friends with Jacob Eames. Eames was a deist and, in practical terms, an atheist. Ridiculing Judson's faith, Eames challenged him with the writings of Voltaire and other French philosophers. When Judson returned home, he told his parents that he, too, had become an atheist. His mother broke into gentle sobs. His father roared and threatened and pounded the furniture.

Judson, then twenty-one, migrated to New York City to establish himself as a playwright. However, hearing tales from the American frontier, he saddled his horse and headed west. One evening, weary from traveling, he stopped at an inn. The proprietor said, "Forgive me, sir, but the only room left—well, it'll be a bit noisy. There's a young fellow next door awfully sick." Too tired to care, Judson took the key.

The night became a nightmare. The tramping of feet coming and going. Muffled voices. Painful groans. Chairs scraping against the floor. Judson felt troubled by it all, and he wondered what his friend Jacob Eames would say about fear, illness, and death.

The next morning, while checking out, he asked about the young man in the next room. The proprietor said, "I thought maybe you'd heard. He died, sir, toward morning. Very young. Not more than your age. Went to that Brown University out East." Judson stiffened. The man continued, "His name was Jacob Eames."

The West suddenly lost its allure, and Judson turned his horse toward home. Soon, he gave his life to Christ and, shortly afterward, devoted himself to missions. On February 6, 1812, Adoniram Judson was commissioned as North America's first foreign missionary. He, his wife, and companions sailed for Burma on February 18.

Prodigals do come home.

28

CALM: Choosing to Abide in the Lord's Mercies

By nature, I'm an anxious person, prone to weep and worry, and too quick to panic, just like a high-strung sheep. Listen to a medley of Scripture verses that have helped me settle my nerves when I've been in pain or panic:

> *Be careful, keep calm and don't be afraid. Do not lose heart.*
> —Isaiah 7:4

> *A man of understanding is of a calm spirit.*
> —Proverbs 17:27

> *You ought to keep calm and to do nothing rash.*
> —Acts 19:36

> *Gideon built an altar for worshipping the Lord and called it, "The Lord Calms Our Fears."*
> —Judges 6:24

[The LORD] calms the storm, so that its waves are still. Then they are glad because they are quiet; so He guides them to their desired haven.

—PSALM 107:29–30

[Jesus] replied, "You of little faith, why are you so afraid?" Then he got up and rebuked the winds and the waves, and it was completely calm.

—MATTHEW 8:26 (NIV)

Lord, my heart is not lifted up, my eyes are not raised too high; I do not occupy myself with things too great and too marvelous for me. But I have calmed and quieted my soul, like a child quieted at its mother's breast; like a child that is quieted is my soul. O Israel, hope in the LORD from this time forth and for evermore.

—PSALM 131:1–3 (RSV)

Calm down, and learn that I am God! All nations on earth will honor me. The LORD All-Powerful is with us. The God of Jacob is our fortress.

—PSALM 46:10–11 (CEV)

Pause, and calmly think of that!

—PSALM 46:3 (AMP)

29

The Multitude of Thy Mercies

Today, focus on your desire to see God be merciful to your child:

Bless and sanctify my child's soul with heavenly blessing, that it may become Thy holy habitation and the seat of Thy eternal glory; and let nothing be found in my child's life which may offend the eyes of Thy majesty. According to the greatness of Thy goodness and the multitude of Thy mercies look upon this one so dear to me, far exiled from Thee in the land of the shadow of death. Protect and preserve the soul of this one, amid so many dangers of corruptible life, and by Thy grace accompanying him, direct him by the way of peace unto his home of perpetual light. Amen.

(Adapted from a prayer by Thomas á Kempis,
Imitation of Christ.)

30

God Devises Means

One day I was surprised to find the following verse, which I had never noticed before and which seemingly appeared just when I needed it: "Yet God does not take away a life; but He devises means, so that His banished ones are not expelled from Him" (2 Samuel 14:14).

Lord,

Please devise means of keeping my child from evading Your grasp. Please devise means of turning him from the broad road to the narrow one. Please devise means of convicting him of sin and guarding him from Satan. Devise means of intervening as necessary to keep him from harming himself and others. Devise means of bringing him into the fullness of the victorious Christian life.

Nudge him, God:
Poke.
Push.

Spur.
Prod.
Goad.
Induce.
And inspire good changes in my child today. Amen.

31

A Prayer from Brother Lawrence

Nicholas Herman, known as Brother Lawrence, was a seventeenth-century French Christian. After his death in 1691, editors compiled his conversations and letters into a little book, *The Practice of the Presence of God* It has become a devotional classic. From its pages I've adapted the following prayer:

> *Lord, You have given* _____ *a good disposition and a good will, but there is in him still a little of the world and a great deal of youth.*
>
> *One does not become holy all at once.*
>
> *Please forgive my child's sins. He shall never do otherwise if You leave him to himself; it is You who must hinder his falling and mend what is amiss.*
>
> *Lord, You have many ways of drawing us to Yourself. Let my son begin to be earnestly devoted to You. Let him cast everything that hinders out of his heart, and may we soon see that change wrought in him that we desire.*
>
> *In Jesus' name. Amen.*

32

Chefoo

M issionaries Alice Taylor and her husband had sent their four children across the vastness of China to boarding school at Chefoo (now Yantai). When the Japanese invaded the region in the early 1940s, reunion became impossible. One day, Alice, already fretting, entered her house just as the paperboy arrived with dramatic news: "Pearl Harbor attacked!" She instantly knew conditions had dramatically worsened for the children, especially because Chefoo lay in the Japanese line of attack.

She later wrote:

> *I remembered the horror stories of Nanking—where all of the young women of that town had been brutally raped. And I thought of our lovely Kathleen, beginning to blossom into womanhood. . . . Great gulping sobs wrenched my whole body. I lay there, gripped by the stories we had heard from refugees—violent deaths, starvation, the conscription of young boys—children—to fight.*
>
> *I thought of ten-year-old Jamie, so conscientious, so even-tempered. "What has happened to Jamie, Lord? Has*

someone put a gun in his hands? Ordered him to the front lines? To death?" Mary and John, so small and so helpless, had always been inseparable. "Merciful God," I cried, "are they even alive?"

As Alice knelt, sobbing and praying, a scene from her childhood came suddenly to mind. Her minister, Pa Ferguson, back in Wilkes-Barre, Pennsylvania, had reminded her of Matthew 6:33: "Seek first the kingdom of God and His righteousness, and all these things shall be added to you." He had rendered the verse, "Alice, if you take care of the things that are dear to God, He will take care of the things dear to you."

Alice now felt God had given her those words just for this day. A deep peace replaced her agony. "This war had not changed God's promise," she said. "With that assurance, I felt the aching weight of fear in my stomach lift."

Alice daily concentrated on taking care of things dear to God: visiting the sick, holding open-air meetings in the villages, delivering babies. Conditions at Chefoo worsened; the Japanese captured the students and herded them into a concentration camp. The war reached Alice's region; all around her bombs fell, rockets exploded. She meanwhile devoted herself to treating the wounded, distributing Scripture to doctors, officers, troops, and students, and to taking care of things important to God.

Years passed.

Then, as I sat one September evening in our home during a faculty meeting, my mind wandered once more to the children. Again I pictured them as I had last seen them, waving goodbye. I heard their voices, faintly, calling excitedly. Then I heard their voices louder. Was I imagining this? No, their voices were real! And they came bursting through the doorway. "Mommy, Daddy, we're home—

we're home!" And they flew into our arms. Our hugs, our shouts filled the room. We couldn't let go of one another. It had been five-and-a-half long, grueling years. Yet there they were—thin, but alive and whole, laughing and crying. Oh, they had grown! But Kathleen still wore the same blue jumper she had worn when I had last seen her.

For our family that advice from Pa Ferguson long ago will always hold special meaning. I pass it along to you, for it is truly so: "If you take care of the things that are dear to God, He will take care of the things dear to you."[10]

33

Lord, I'm Tired of Waiting!

How hard it is to wait on the Lord, yet how often we must do this for our prodigals!

We must give God time to work in our children's hearts. After all, it's taken Him years to do much with us, and He isn't finished yet. Perhaps, from His perspective, we're a bit more of a disappointment to Him, considering our age and experience, than our children are to us.

In any case, the Bible teaches that trials are God's way of maturing us. The spinning core of maturity is patience and perseverance.

James said, "The testing of your faith develops perseverance. Perseverance must finish its work so that you may be mature" (James 1:3–4, niv).

Paul wrote, "We also glory in tribulations, knowing that tribulation produces perseverance; and perseverance, character" (Romans 5:3–4).

Through the years, I've collected some helpful insights about patiently waiting on the Lord. Perhaps they'll encourage you, too.

Patience means living out the belief that God orders everything for the spiritual good of his children.

—J. I. Packer

Grin and bear it is old-fashioned advice, but sing and bear it is a great deal better.

—Charles H. Spurgeon

Patience does not just grin and bear things, stoic-like, but accepts them cheerfully as therapeutic workouts planned by a heavenly trainer who is resolved to get you up to full fitness.

—J. I. Packer

Are we prepared to take the awful patient ways of God? We must not be infected by the world's valuation of either speed or success.

—John B. Phillips

The trouble is that I'm in a hurry, but God isn't.

—Phillips Brooks, Boston pastor, when asked the reason for his agitation

I'm extraordinarily patient, provided I get my own way in the end.

—Margaret Thatcher

Patience and passage of time do more than strength and fury.

—Jean de la Fontaine, poet

The two most powerful warriors are patience and time.

—Leo Tolstoy, novelist

Our patience will achieve more than our force.

—Edmund Burke

With time and patience the mulberry leaf becomes a silk gown.

—Chinese proverb

Wait on the Lord; be of good courage, and He shall strengthen your heart; wait, I say, on the Lord!

—Psalm 27:14

34

Make Him a Captive, Lord

I've found great strength in the powerful hymn of the blind Scottish pastor George Matheson. "Make Me a Captive, Lord" is a good prayer not only for me but for my loved ones. The first verse says:

> *Make me a captive, Lord, and then I shall be free.*
> *Force me to render up my sword, and I shall conqueror be.*
> *I sink in life's alarms when by myself I stand;*
> *Imprison me within Thine arms,*
> *and strong shall be my hand.*

The hymn reminds me of these words in Isaiah and then leads me to pray:

> *The LORD still waits for you to come to him so he can show*
> *you his love and compassion. For the LORD is a faithful God.*
> *Blessed are those who wait for him to help them.*
> —ISAIAH 30:18 (NLT)

Lord, thank You for waiting on my child to come to You. Please conquer him that You might bless him. I trust You to be faithful to Your promises, and I will wait on You to help us.

It is easy to convert Matheson's hymn to a prayer:

Make _____ a captive, Lord, and then he shall be free;

    Force him to render up his sword, and he shall conqueror be;
    He sinks in life's alarms when by himself he stands;
    Imprison him within Thine arms, and strong shall be his hands.

35

When Jesus Had Trouble with His Children

Jesus' special children—His disciples—caused Him a great deal of sadness. Especially Peter, but Jesus prayed for him, and he eventually turned out all right.

If Jesus had trouble with His kids, it shouldn't surprise us that we sometimes encounter the same thing. Why not take a page from His Book and adapt the Lord's words as a prayer of your own?

> *The Lord said, "Simon, Simon! Indeed, Satan has asked for you, that he may sift you as wheat. But I have prayed for you, that your faith should not fail; and when you have returned to Me, strengthen your brethren."*
>
> *But, he said to Him, "Lord, I am ready to go with You, both to prison and to death."*
>
> *Then, He said, "I tell you, Peter, the rooster shall not crow this day before you will deny three times that you know Me."*
>
> —Luke 22:31–34

Lord, . . . Satan has desired my child, to sift him like wheat. But I pray for him, that his faith should not fail. May he return to You, and afterward be a strength to many.

36

Descend and Melt

During a sermon on Thursday evening, August 21, 1890, London's prince of preachers, Charles H. Spurgeon, quoted a stanza of an old, now-forgotten hymn. These simple words have served as a perfect prayer for my children—and for myself.

> *Is there a heart that will not bend*
> *To Thy divine control?*
> *Descend, O sovereign love, descend,*
> *And melt that stubborn soul!*

37

A Prayer from Augustine's *Confessions*

Aurelius Augustine, born A.D. 354, was a brilliant but utterly immoral young man. For three decades, his mother, Monica, prayed for him, following him from Africa to Italy, weeping, pleading, and assaulting heaven with perpetual missiles of prayer. The Lord finally answered in wondrous ways, for Monica's wayward son eventually became one of the most influential figures in Christian history.

As my child headed to the university, I found great strength in reading Augustine's autobiography, *Confessions*, which he wrote in the form of a prayer. Using phrases in that book, I composed this petition:

> Lord,
>
> *Thy omnipotence is not far from us, even when we are far from Thee, and Thy faithful mercy hovers over us from afar.*
>
> *During this unstable period of life, please keep back _____ from strange sins. Stretch forth Thy hand from above and draw up his soul from darkness. Even now pierce his heart with Thy love, guide him by inward stings*

> *and by the secret impulses of Thy providence, and set his*
> *shameful errors before his face that he might see and hate*
> *them.*
>
> *Go on, O Lord, and act: stir him up and call him back;*
> *inflame him and draw him to Thee; stir him up and grow*
> *sweet to him; let him now love Thee; let him run to Thee."*

Monica waited for years for Augustine to come to Christ, but she would have quickly told you that it was worth it. Wait on the Lord; give Him time to work.

38

Answers Beyond Death

One evening at a banquet, Pam Frye, a children's pastor from Battlefield Parkway Church of the Nazarene in Fort Oglethorpe, Georgia, told me that she is one of eleven children, many of whom strayed far from God during their adolescent and early adult years. Her father, however, was a man of prayer who begged the Lord for his children to all be saved and happy in Jesus Christ.[12]

"He prayed all his children into the kingdom," Pam said, "the last four coming to the Lord after his death."

D. L. Moody once wrote, "Though we may not live to see the answer to our prayers, if we cry mightily to God, the answer will come."

E. M. Bounds, minister and Civil War chaplain, who authored eight classic books on prayer, wrote:

> *Prayers are deathless. The lips that uttered them may close*
> *in death, the heart that felt them may cease to beat, but the*
> *prayers live before God. God's heart is set on them and*
> *prayers outlive the lives of those who uttered them; outlive*
> *a generation, outlive an age, outlive a world. . . . Fortunate*

are they whose fathers and mother have left them a wealthy
patrimony of prayer.[13]

Ruth Bell Graham, wife of evangelist Billy Graham, once said, "I prayed to the Lord day and night, month after month, year after year. Was God deaf? Is He indifferent? No. He had His reasons. Something to accomplish in the heart of that loved prodigal. Something to accomplish in my heart. Prayers are answered even after we're gone."

William Grimshaw was born in rural England in 1708, educated at Cambridge, and ordained as a minister in 1731—without knowing Christ. Three years later, while pastoring in Todmorden, he felt deep concern over his soul. He ceased his hunting, fishing, card-playing, and merrymaking and began pleading with God for light. After several more years, the scales completely fell from his eyes. The gospel became real to him, and the Bible came alive. He told a friend that, "If God had drawn up his Bible to heaven and sent me down another, it could not have been newer to me."

Grimshaw moved to Haworth in Yorkshire and began a twenty-one-year ministry. Had he been in London, claim his biographers, he would have become one of the most famous preachers of the eighteenth century. The town of Haworth was rough and uncivilized, a long, narrow village of brown stone. The main street was so steep that carriages traveled it at their own risk. Here Grimshaw labored in obscurity but with great zeal. He gathered listeners wherever he could—in barns, fields, and quarries—and pressed them with the gospel.

He once said, "When I die I shall then have my greatest grief and my greatest joy—my greatest grief that I have done so little for Jesus, and my greatest joy that Jesus has done so much for me."

Grimshaw's heart broke over his son, John, who rejected Christ and lived a careless, intemperate life. When John visited his father as he lay dying, Grimshaw said to his son, "Take care what you do, for you are not fit to die." Those words haunted the young man.

One day, John met a Haworth inhabitant who said, "I see you are riding the old parson's horse."

"Yes," replied John. "Once he carried a great saint, and now he carries a great sinner."

However, not for long. For John soon heeded his father's dying pleas and gave his heart to Christ. He died shortly afterward on May 17, 1766, saying. "What will my old father say when he sees I have got to heaven?"

How about *Hallelujah!?*[14]

39

Life's Waiting Rooms

Recently I found an interesting dichotomy in the Psalms that illustrates our struggle when we find ourselves in life's waiting rooms. On the one hand, the psalmists extol the virtue of waiting on the Lord:

> *Wait for the LORD; be strong and take heart and wait for the LORD.*
>
> —PSALM 27:14 (NIV)

> *We wait in hope for the LORD; he is our help and our shield.*
>
> —33:20 (NIV)

> *Be still before the LORD and wait patiently for him; do not fret when men succeed in their ways.*
>
> —37:7 (NIV)

> *Those who hope in the LORD will inherit the land.*
>
> —37:9 (NIV)

Wait for the LORD and keep his way. He will exalt you.
—37:34 (NIV)

I wait for you, O LORD; you will answer, O LORD my God.
—38:15 (NIV)

I wait for the LORD, my soul waits, and in his word I put my hope. My soul waits for the LORD more than watchmen wait for the morning, more than watchmen wait for the morning.
—130:5–6 (NIV)

Yet another phrase occurs with even greater frequency throughout the Psalms. The same authors who tell us to wait on the Lord also wonder . . .

How long, O LORD, how long?
—6:3 (NIV)

How long, O LORD? Will you forget me forever? How long will you hide your face from me? How long must I wrestle with my thoughts and every day have sorrow in my heart? How long will my enemy triumph over me?
—13:1–2 (NIV)

O LORD, how long will you look on?
—35:17 (NIV)

We are given no miraculous signs; no prophets are left, and none of us knows how long this will be. How long will the enemy mock you, O God?
—74:9–10 (NIV)

O Lᴏʀᴅ God Almighty, how long will your anger smolder against the prayers of your people?

—80:4 (ɴɪᴠ)

How long, O Lᴏʀᴅ? Will you hide yourself forever? How long will your wrath burn like fire? Remember how fleeting is my life.

—89:46–47 (ɴɪᴠ)

Relent, O Lᴏʀᴅ! How long will it be?

—90:13 (ɴɪᴠ)

How long will the wicked, O Lᴏʀᴅ, how long will the wicked be jubilant?

—94:3 (ɴɪᴠ)

How long must your servant wait?

—119:84 (ɴɪᴠ)

We can relate to this dilemma. On one hand, we're told to wait on the Lord, and on the other hand we are, by nature, impatient. When we feel in distress, in pain, or in rough circumstances, something within us cries out, "Lord, how long?"

Notice two things. On the one hand, God never rebuked His impatient people for asking, "How long?" In fact, He even honored their question by including it in Scripture. On the other hand, He also never answered their question. Instead He directed them to wait on His timing—and in the meanwhile, He gave them a word of hope. In the words of Isaiah:

Since ancient times no one has heard,
no ear has perceived,
no eye has seen any God besides you,
who acts on behalf of those who wait for him.
—Isᴀɪᴀʜ 64:4 (ɴɪᴠ)

40

Aligning Life's Circumstances

One of the most interesting aspects of Jesus Christ's life and ministry was His sense of timing. Recently, I noticed how the Lord Jesus seemed to delay His very coming to this earth.

Beginning with the words in Genesis 3:15, God promised He would send the Anointed One, a Messiah, to redeem His people from their sin. Abraham was told he would become the forefather of One through whom all the world would be blessed. Jacob said this Messiah would be of the tribe of Judah. Moses told us He would be a great prophet. We're told He would be of the lineage of David and would occupy the throne of David forever. The prophet Isaiah spoke frequently of this coming Messiah.

Micah predicted He would be born in Bethlehem, and Zechariah said He would enter Jerusalem riding on a donkey. Line upon line, precept upon precept, prophecy upon prophecy, the details of the Messiah's life and mission were given—more than three hundred separate prophecies given over fifteen hundred years.

All Israel waited eagerly for this Redeemer. The Old Testament wore to a close. The latter prophets preached their messages—Haggai, Zechariah, and finally Malachi, who ended his book with the words "lest I come and smite the earth with a curse."

Everyone waited, but the Messiah did not appear. Instead, Alexander the Great blazed across Europe and Asia like a meteor, dominating the world. Still no Messiah.

After Alexander's early death, the little nation of Israel was brutalized by the Syrian dynasty of Seleucid and by its tyrant, Antiochus IV. The years became decades, and the decades became centuries. Still no Messiah. Generations came and perished. Eras came and went. Still no Messiah.

According to Jewish scholar Alfred Edersheim, great discussions took place among the ancient rabbis of Israel on the question, "What delayeth His coming?" Hope dwindled. Edersheim wrote: "After years of unrelieved sufferings, the Synagogue had to acknowledge that, one by one, all the terms had passed, and as despair settled on the heart of Israel, it came to be generally thought that the time of Messiah's Advent could not be known beforehand, and that speculation on the subject was dangerous, sinful, even damnable."

What was God's perspective on this issue? Galatians 4:4 says, "When the time had fully come, God sent his Son" (NIV). Looking back on it from the perspective of the ages, we can see that Jesus Christ came at just the right moment in human history.

He came at the right *religious moment*. Four things occurred in the religious history of Israel between the Old and New Testaments. First, the Jews finally adhered to monotheism: the belief in one God. Second, Jewish scholars compiled and canonized their Scriptures, establishing what today is called the Old Testament. Third, during this period, the Hebrew Scriptures were translated into the more universal Greek. Fourth, during the Babylonian captivity, the Jews were scattered across the known world. As a result, when the New Testament apostles went forth preaching, they found that their fellow Jews had already acquainted the world with monotheism and with the law of God, thus paving the way for the message of the gospel.

The Lord Jesus also came at the right *cultural moment*. The most dramatic event between the Old and New Testaments was the mete-oric rise of Alexander the Great, who swept over Europe and Asia, transforming the world into a world of one tongue: Greek. When the apostles went forth to preach the gospel, they preached in Greek. They had no need for language schools, no need for translators, no language barriers.

Jesus came at just the right *political moment*. The dominant world power at the time of Christ's birth was the Roman Empire, which provided two things critical to the success of the gospel: a fantastic system of roads to every corner of the empire and an era of worldwide peace.

It was the only time in human history when all these conditions came together at once. In large measure, these factors made possible the rapid spread of the gospel in the days following our Lord's resur-rection.

What a great lesson! It teaches us the power of patience regarding life events. We must trust His timing and our hearts must give Him time to align the circumstances for our good.

Why are so many of my prayer requests not immediately an-swered? Perhaps God is patiently waiting until all the circumstances are correctly aligned for the widest possible fulfillment of those re-quests or aspirations. The same keen, impeccable sense of divine tim-ing that sent Jesus into the world at the optimum moment for the propagation of the gospel is the same keen, impeccable sense of divine timing that answers our prayers and directs our lives.

The Lord Jesus Christ is Alpha and Omega, the Beginning and the End, the First and the Last. He knows the end from the begin-ning, and sometimes so-called delays occur in life because God is aligning circumstances for our benefit. We have to wait on Him and trust Him, knowing His timing is as perfect as He is.

41

Make Him Clean

Today, focus on your desire to see your child turn from his sin and be cleansed completely from it:

Father,
   Draw _____ *out of the unhealthy*
environments around him and bring him to a holy place in
life.
   Sprinkle clean water on him and make him clean.
   Cleanse him from all filthiness and from all his idols, and
give him a new heart. Put a new spirit within him. Take
away the heart of stone, and give him a tender heart. Put
Your Spirit within him, and cause him to walk in Your
statutes and to keep Your judgments. Deliver him from all
his uncleanness, and multiply Your blessings to him.
   Not for our sake, O Father, but for Your glory I ask this,
and on Your grace I lean.
   Then we shall know that You are the Lord.

(Adapted from Ezekiel 36.)

42

A Medley of Scriptures
about Leaning on the Promises

Today, focus on the promises of God:

God is not a man, that He should lie. It is impossible for God to lie. Has He said, and will He not do it? Or has He spoken, and will He not make it good? He who calls you is faithful, who also will do it. There has not failed one word of all His good promise, which He promised. Not a word failed of any good thing which the Lord had spoken to the house of Israel. All came to pass. You know in all your hearts and in all your souls that not one thing has failed of all the good things which the Lord your God spoke concerning you. All have come to pass for you; not one word of them has failed. Therefore take heart, men, for I believe God that it will be just as it was told me. For all the promises of God in Him are Yes, and in Him Amen, to the glory of God through us.

(Numbers 23:19; Hebrews 6:18; Numbers 23:19;
1 Thessalonians 5:24; 1 Kings 8:56; Joshua 21:45, 23:14;
Acts 27:25; 2 Corinthians 1:20.)

I have thumbed my Bible many a year; I have never yet thumbed a broken promise. The promises have all been kept to me; not one good thing has failed.

—CHARLES H. SPURGEON

43

God Isn't Discouraged

Don't give up on your kids, never stop praying, and don't give in to discouragement, for all discouragement comes from the Devil. Those of us who were problem kids ourselves—and those who have troubled children now—know it takes time, love, prayer, patience, understanding, support, and lots of faith in a God who has warned us against despair. Put the following verses side by side in your heart, and learn to lean:

Then they journeyed from Mount Hor by the Way of the Red Sea, to go around the land of Edom; and the soul of the people became very discouraged on the way. —NUMBERS 21:4	*"Have I not commanded you? Be strong and courageous. Do not be terrified; do not be discouraged, for the LORD your God will be with you wherever you go."* —JOSHUA 1:9 (NIV)
For when they went up to the Valley of Eshcol and saw the land, they discouraged the heart of the children of Israel, so that they did not go into the land which the LORD had given them. —NUMBERS 32:9	*"Be strong and courageous, and do the work. Do not be afraid or discouraged, for the LORD God, my God, is with you. He will not fail you or forsake you until all the work . . . is finished."* —1 CHRONICLES 28:20 (NIV)
Then the peoples around them set out to discourage the people of Judah and make them afraid to go on building. —EZRA 4:4 (NIV)	*This is what the LORD says to you: "Do not be afraid or discouraged because of this vast army. For the battle is not yours, but God's."* —2 CHRONICLES 20:15 (NIV)
But now trouble comes to you, and you are discouraged; it strikes you, and you are dismayed. Should not your piety be your confidence and your blameless ways your hope? —JOB 4:5–6 (NIV)	*For everything that was written in the past was written to teach us, so that through endurance and the encouragement of the Scriptures we might have hope. . . . God [gives] endurance and encouragement.* —ROMANS 15:4–5 (NIV)

During our own period of anxious waiting, one primary source of encouragement has enabled us to press on: God's reliable Word, "the encouragement of the Scriptures." In the Bible, God tells us to pray for our children. Consider some of the verses that helped my wife, Katrina, and me cast out discouragement and keep on praying:

As for me, far be it from me that I should sin against the LORD in ceasing to pray for you.

—1 SAMUEL 12:23

*Pour out your heart like water
in the presence of the LORD . . .
for the lives of your children.*
—LAMENTATIONS 2:19 (NIV)

*They shall come back from the land of the enemy.
There is hope in your future, says the LORD,
That your children will come back to their own border.*
—JEREMIAH 31:16–17

I will contend with those who contend with you, and I will save your children.

—ISAIAH 49:25 (NRSV)

I prayed for this child, and the LORD has granted me what I asked of him.

—1 SAMUEL 1:27 (NIV)

Always pray, and never become discouraged. . . . Keep on praying and never give up.

—LUKE 18:1 (TEV, CEV)

God's encouragement doesn't fluctuate with changing winds or shifting tides. He doesn't tie His enabling to circumstances, and His morale doesn't depend on moons or moods. Even when we're faithless, He remains faithful, so recognize discouragement as a guest that has overstayed its welcome and that cannot abide the presence of the heavenly Father. Choose faith over fear, prayer over panic, and abiding trust over anxious care. It isn't a matter of getting a grip on the situation; it's a matter of letting God get a grip on you.

44

God's Recipe for Prayer

If you want to grow in faith and prayer, read E. M. Bounds, the Civil War era preacher who became the greatest American writer on the subject. His numerous books will convict, motivate, and instruct you in becoming a prayer warrior for your loved one. Here's an excerpt that has encouraged me to lean on the Lord.

> *The Word of God is the fulcrum upon which the lever of prayer is placed, and by which things are mightily moved. God has committed Himself, His purpose, and His promise to prayer. His Word becomes the basis, the inspiration of our praying, and there are circumstances under which, by importance [unrelenting] prayer, we may obtain an addition or an enlargement of His promises. It is said of the old saints that they, "through faith obtained promises." There would seem to be in prayer the capacity of getting even beyond His promise, into the very presence of God Himself.*
>
> *Jacob wrestled not so much with a promise as with the Promiser. We must take hold of the Promiser, lest the promise prove nugatory [weak]. Prayer may well be*

defined as the force which vitalizes and energizes the Word of God by taking hold of God Himself. By taking hold of the Promiser, prayer reissues and makes personal the promise. "There is none . . . that stirreth up himself to take hold of Thee [Me]," is God's sad lament (Isaiah 64:7, KJV). "Let him take hold of My strength, that he may make peace with Me" (Isaiah 27:5) is God's recipe for prayer. . . .

The Word of God is a great help in prayer. If it be lodged and written in our hearts, it will form an outflowing current of prayer, full and irresistible. Promises, stored in the heart, are to be the fuel from which prayer receives life and warmth, just as the coal, stored in the earth, ministers to our comfort on stormy days and wintry nights.

The Word of God is the food by which prayer is nourished and made strong. Prayer, like man, cannot live by bread alone, "but by every word which proceedeth out of the mouth of the Lord."

45

Hedge Him in Behind and Before

Today, focus on your desire to see your child recognize God's presence:

O Lord,

You have searched and known my child, wherever he is at any given moment.

You know when he sits down and gets up. You read his thoughts.

You comprehend his path and are acquainted with all his ways.

Please hedge him in behind and before, and lay Your hand upon him.

Where can he go from Your Spirit? Where can he flee from Your presence?

If he ascends to heaven, You are there. If he makes his bed in hell, behold, You are there.

If he takes the wings of the morning and dwells far away, even there Your right hand will hold him.

He is fearfully and wonderfully made. Your eyes saw his

unformed substance, being yet unformed, and in Your book were all his days recorded when as yet there were none of them. How precious are Your thoughts toward my child, O God!

Search _____, *O God, and know his heart. Try him, and know his anxieties. See if there is any wicked way in him, and lead him in the way everlasting.*

(Adapted from Psalm 139.)

46

Carry It on to Completion

You can lean heavily on the book of Philippians, and it will not weaken or stagger under your weight. Though its author wrote it while in prison, it bursts with joy and brims with optimism. Here's a prayer gleaned from phrases in the first chapter:

> *Lord, I thank You for_____, being confident of this, that You who have begun a good work in him will carry it on to completion until the day of Christ. It is right for me to pray this, because I have him in my heart. You know how greatly I long for this child with the affection of Christ. I pray that his love may abound more and more in knowledge and discernment, that he may approve the things that are excellent. Make him sincere and without offense until the day of Christ, being filled with the fruits of righteousness to Your glory and praise.*

> (Adapted from Philippians 1:3–11.)

47

Blessings from Burdens

God has meant this trial to strengthen my faith, to drive me deeper into His heart, and to expand my empathy. I've bonded with other parents whose kids are going through difficult times, and I can better relate to those in pain. I have a list of prodigals for whom I daily intercede. My prayer life has made a quantum leap, and I'm slowly learning the secrets of finding refuge in God alone.

Occasional short-term disruptions have occurred in my ministry, but the long-term benefits have already indirectly touched my congregation. I'm exceedingly eager to fully emerge from the valley but, until then, God will not abandon me, nor will His promises fail. Sometimes I must minister in sheer faith, preaching when my own heart is breaking and comforting others when I'm the one in greater need. Amy Carmichael put it well when she described the panicked disciples on the waters of Galilee.

> *Looking back on that night the most vivid memory must*
> *have been, not the darkness or the weariness, not the great*
> *wind and the rough sea, but the blessed Morning Aid that*
> *came before the morning. Let us not make too much of the*

storm in the night. . . . The wind was contrary unto them then, perhaps it is contrary to us now. But just when things were hardest in that tiredest of all times (between 2 a.m. and 6 a.m.), just then, He came.

The Lord is near. Even when we feel unable to minister to others, He can minister through us. And that's the way it should be, anyway.[15]

48

Help Him Praise You

Today, focus on your desire to see your child praise God:

Lord, one generation praises Your works to another and declares Your mighty acts. You are gracious and full of compassion, slow to anger and great in mercy. You are good to all, and Your tender mercies are over all Your works. You uphold all who fall and raise up all who are bowed down. . . .

Deliver my son, O Lord, from evil men. Preserve him from violent men, who plan evil things in their hearts. Keep my child, O Lord, from the hands of the wicked, who would make his steps stumble.

My spirit is overwhelmed within me. Cause him to know the way in which he should walk. Teach him to do Your will. Lead him in the land of uprightness. Revive him, O Lord, for Your name's sake. Bless my child.

(Adapted from Psalms 145:4, 8–9, 14;
140:1–2, 4; 143:4, 8, 10–11; 147:13.)

49

In Spite of Himself

John Donne was himself a prodigal, born in London in 1573. Brought up a Roman Catholic, he lived a reckless life for many years. His sermons and prayers are now classics. I have adapted one of his prayers as my own for our children.

> *O Lord, You have set up many candlesticks and kindled many lamps for my child, but he has either blown them out or carried them to guide him in forbidden ways. You have given him a desire of knowledge, and some means to it, and some possession of it; but he has armed himself with weapons against You. Yet, O God, have mercy upon him. For Your own sake have mercy on him. Let not sin frustrate Your purpose in his life. But let him, in spite of himself, be of so much use to Your glory that by Your mercy other sinners may see how much sin You will pardon.*

My Favorite Insight on Prayer

Bishop Joseph Hall—an ardent seventeenth-century Anglican once imprisoned in the Tower of London for his Puritan leanings—spent his final years on a small farm in the English countryside, where he wrote devotional classics that will live forever. Here is what he said about prayer.

> *An arrow, if it be drawn up but a little way, goes not far;*
> *but, if it be pulled up to the head, flies swiftly and pierces deep.*
> *Thus prayer, if it be only dribbled forth from careless lips, falls*
> *at our feet. It is the strength of [discharge] and strong desire*
> *which sends it to heaven, and makes it pierce the clouds. It is*
> *not the arithmetic of our prayers, how many they are; not the*
> *rhetoric of our prayers, how eloquent they be; nor the geometry*
> *of our prayers, how long they be; nor the music of our prayers,*
> *how sweet our voice may be; nor the logic of our prayers, how*
> *argumentative they may be; nor the method of our prayers,*
> *how orderly they may be; nor even the divinity of our prayers,*
> *how good the doctrine may be;—which God cares for.*
> *Fervency of spirit is that which availeth much.*

51

Advice from a Psychologist

Another book that has revived me when I feel my emotions slipping is *Parenting the Prodigal*, by S. Rutherford McDill, Jr. Consider these few paragraphs:

> *Stay calm. . . . Your prodigal wants you to be hysterical;*
> *that's his payoff. Don't give it. This refusal gives your*
> *prodigal the sense that you are basically grounded, unshaken,*
> *in control. If you lose your cool you may exchange words*
> *that will wound your relationship. If you feel as if you are*
> *about to explode, take a break. Get away from the scene and*
> *collect yourself. Do some deep breathing, listen to relaxing*
> *music, go for a walk or run. Let your surging adrenaline*
> *return to rest levels. The aim is to model self-control. . . .*
>
> *When times get especially bad, the thought of a porch*
> *light and an open door may be the only direction-finding*
> *device your prodigal has. . . . Knowing that the door is*
> *always open, the porch light is on, and the welcome mat is*
> *out will draw your child home like a magnet.*[16]

52

Treading the Grapes

Times of testing are times of learning, of growing, of inwardly progressing in our souls. Whenever we face fear and heartbreak, our hearts can become tenderly receptive to new insights from God.

What an opportunity to have daily devotions!

My daily quiet times with God help me through every single difficulty I face. Consider three insights I picked up from others about the process of personal growth through daily Bible reading and prayer, especially the power of combining the two, like nitric acid and glycerol.

From George Mueller:

> *The first thing I did, after having asked in a few words
> the Lord's blessing upon His precious Word, was to begin
> to meditate on the Word of God, searching as it were into
> every verse to get blessing out of it; not for the sake of public
> ministry of the Word, not for the sake of preaching on what
> I had meditated upon, but for the sake of obtaining food for*

my soul. The result I have found to be almost invariably this, that after a very few minutes my soul has been led to confession, or to thanksgiving, or to supplication; so that, though I did not, as it were, give myself to prayer, but to meditation, yet it turned almost immediately more or less into prayer.

From Charles H. Spurgeon:

Pray over the Scripture, it is as the treading of grapes in the wine vat, the threshing of corn on the barn floor, the melting of gold from the ore.

From Samuel Clark:

A thorough acquaintance with the promises would be of the greatest advantage in prayer. . . . With how much satisfaction may [the Christian] offer up the several desires of his heart when he reflects upon the texts wherein those very mercies are promised! And with what fervor of spirit and strength of faith may he enforce his prayers, by pleading the several gracious promises which are expressly to his case!

Why not put down this book and pick up your Bible? Find a verse to claim right now for yourself and for your loved one.

53

A Copenhagen Prayer

I awoke early one morning in Copenhagen, and I calculated that the clock must just then be striking midnight back in the university town where my daughter was. For no real reason, panic swept over me. I threw on some clothes and a coat and braved the early morning chill to find a phone booth.

She didn't answer.

Returning to my room, I fought to subdue my rising, irrational fears. In my prayer journal, I jotted down seven words that became a daily prayer for her for several years.

> *Lord,*
> *Give my child . . .*
> *Discernment and discretion,*
> *Discipline and diligence,*
> *Direction in life,*
> *Devotion to Christ and delight in Your Word,*
> *In Jesus' name. Amen.*

We must learn to be sensitive to the Holy Spirit for the prayers He wants to give us, and then we must pray them in faith, learning to trust Him even if we're thousands of miles away from the recipient of our prayers.

54

Talking to Yourself

During a particularly stubborn bout of pessimism, I went away for a few days with a book titled, *Spiritual Depression: Its Causes and Cure,* by Martyn Lloyd-Jones. One of the chapters suggests that we often get into emotional trouble when we *listen* to ourselves instead of *talking* to ourselves.

I had been listening intently to my own inner voices of fear, sadness, worry, and alarm, when I should have been sitting myself down, taking myself in hand, and giving myself a good talking-to.

Acting on Lloyd-Jones' advice, I started reminding myself of God's promises, writing them in my journal, sliding them under the glass on my desk, and posting them on my dashboard so I could quote them while driving to the office. In short, I started talking to myself instead of listening to all my faithless inner voices of alarm.

It worked.

The same thing worked for David. Recently, while studying 1 Samuel, I noticed that, in chapter 23, David, a young man at the time, had fallen into deep trouble. Several disasters had befallen him, and he felt distraught. In verse 16, his friend Jonathan came along and "strengthened his hand in God." In other words, Jonathan encouraged him, gave him a pep talk, and helped him regain his strength and composure.

Seven chapters later, in 1 Samuel 30, David again found himself in soul-crushing distress. This time Jonathan couldn't come to him, and he had no one to comfort or encourage him, no one to give him a pep talk. So, what did he do? First Samuel 30:6 says, "David strengthened *himself* in the Lord his God" (emphasis added).

This is an important technique to learn. Sometimes we have no one around to uplift or encourage us, no one on whom we can lean. In such times we must learn to encourage *ourselves* in the Lord, to give ourselves pep talks, to talk ourselves out of discouragement and de-spair.

As you work through this book, copy down the sentences, truths, and phrases that seem most helpful to you. Put them on your mirror, your dashboard, your nightstand, your refrigerator door, in your purse or pocket, or under the glass on your desk. Feed your faith! Remind yourself of God's truth. Learn to stop listening to the inner voices of apprehension; instead, preach to yourself the affirmations of God.

Talking to yourself isn't a sign of insanity; sometimes, it's a cure for it.

55

What to Say When You Talk to Yourself

Troubled parents generally love Psalm 103, a cloudless chapter devoted exclusively to counting our blessings and lauding our Lord. It contains nothing but praise. No dismal moods, no requests, no petitions, and no problems. Sometimes we need to breathe such bracing air.

In this psalm, King David used his well-honed technique of talking to himself to speak the truth to his soul about his blessings and benefits in God. In addressing his own soul, he wrote:

> *Bless the LORD, O my soul;*
> *And all that is within me, bless His holy name!*
> *Bless the LORD, O my soul,*
> *And forget not all His benefits:*
> *Who forgives all your iniquities,*
> *Who heals all your diseases,*
> *Who redeems your life from destruction,*
> *Who crowns you with loving kindness and tender mercies,*
> *Who satisfies your mouth with good things.*

—VERSES 1–5

Paraphrasing his words for my own use, I would say: "Self, you've been in the dumps long enough—fretting, fearful, fainthearted. It's time to shake it off. Cheer up! Remember God's blessings. Don't forget His benefits toward you. You've forgotten His divine presence. You've overlooked His promises. Enough of that! Acknowledge the Lord's blessing, O my soul, and all that is within me—from head to foot—bless His holy name."

David then takes us on a little *tour* of the benefits and blessings enjoyed by God's children.

The first stop is the *courthouse*, where we remind ourselves that the Lord has declared us "Not guilty!" by virtue of Christ's sacrifice on Calvary: "Bless the LORD, O my soul . . . who forgives all your iniquities" (verses 2–3). Later, in verses 11–12, he uses a graphic comparison to underscore the immensity of God's forgiveness, telling us that as far as the east is from the west, so far has He removed our sins from us.

A law student visited me recently. He had fallen into deep and prolonged sin at his fraternity and felt smothered in guilt. His face bore signs of weary despair, and his eyes could hardly look at me. "I've confessed and confessed my sins," he said sadly, "but I can't imagine God has forgiven me."

I picked up my book of daily Scripture readings and turned to the page on God's forgiveness. "Read these verses to me," I said. He began crying as the Scripture's powerful truths flushed the hopelessness from his soul. By the end of the verses, he had begun to sense that he could be clean again, that God would forgive to the uttermost.

Next, Psalm 103 takes us to a *hospital*. It reminds us that God not only forgives all our sins, but also heals all our diseases. I believe this refers to every type of disease—physical, emotional, and spiritual. I don't accept the assertion that God *always* heals *all* our physical diseases in this life—that runs counter to the overall teachings of Scripture and to the actual experiences of Christians. Even the apostle Paul was not healed of his thorn in the flesh, mentioned in 2 Corinthians

12:7–10. Nevertheless, God can give physical healing in answer to prayer, and He often does.

But what of Paul *now?* If we had a telescope that could gaze into heaven, into the city of God, we would see Paul healthy, happy, and disease free. Heaven harbors no cancer, no heart disease, no high blood pressure. God will either heal us in this life or He will heal us through the process of death; in either case, the Bible says that "by His wounds we are healed" (Isaiah 53:5, NIV).

In our tour of God's blessings, the psalmist next takes us by the *pit* from which we have been saved: "who redeems your life from the pit" (Psalm 103:4, NIV). In Biblical times, men dug deep holes in the desolate sands to find water. Occasionally these cisterns found a secondary use as one-man prisons. Job accused his so-called comforters of wanting to plunge him into an emotional slime pit (see Job 9:31). Whenever we feel downcast or depressed, we should stroll by the pit and remind ourselves of God's redemption from it.

From the pit, we go to the *palace* in Psalm 103:4: "who crowns you with loving kindness and tender mercies." Just imagine an invisible crown on your head. When we come to Christ, He crowns us with His infinite love and compassion. We are seated with Christ "in the heavenly realms" (Ephesians 2:6, NIV), reigning in life through that one Man (see Romans 5:17). He wore a crown of thorns that we might wear a crown of glory, and each of our lives as believers is crowned with His love.

Our last stop is the *bank* where we are reminded that God has promised to meet all our needs: "who satisfies your desires with good things" (Psalm 103:5, NIV). This implies we have certain needs and desires. Financial needs. Physical needs. Relational needs. A need for inner peace and strength. For guidance. For His help with our children. When we seek first God's kingdom and righteousness, all these things will be given to us. When we make Him our shepherd, we shall not want. When we delight ourselves in the Lord, He will give us the desires of our heart.

No wonder the psalmist saw a cloudless sky that day! No wonder he said to himself,

> *Bless the LORD, O my soul;*
> *And all that is within me, bless His holy name!*
> —PSALM 103:1

Today, talk to yourself.
Today, praise.

56

Prayers from the Prophet Hosea

Perhaps those with prodigals learn more from Scripture than anyone else; we understand the biblical story from the divine perspective of a grieving Father. Every book takes on a new light.

Read Hosea, for example. This poor man had a prodigal wife, and the situation seemed hopeless. But Hosea never gave up. His book is filled at once with both grief and compassion, with both heartbreaking sorrow and a fierce determination for reclamation. In the process, Hosea gives us much fodder for prayer:

> *Heavenly Father, sow righteousness into the soul of my child; reap mercy in his life. Break up the fallow ground of his heart, and may he seek You till You come and rain righteousness upon him. . . .*
>
> *Draw him with gentle cords, with bands of love. Heal his backsliding. Love him freely. Revive his heart as with dew. May he become as pleasant as the lily, as straight as the cedars of Lebanon, as fruitful as an olive tree.*

(Adapted from 10:12, 11:4, 14:4–5.)

57

Short but Powerful

Sometimes, God calls us to extended periods of prayer for our prodigal; sometimes, we can do our prayer work in a much shorter time. Some of Jesus' prayers were quite brief, but very deep and powerful. The following prayers are short, but none in Scripture is better for your child:

Create in _____ a clean heart, O God, and renew a steadfast spirit within him
   Send out Your light and Your truth! Let them lead him. Let them bring him to Your holy hill.

(Adapted from Psalms 51:10, 43:3.)

58

A Potpourri of Help

Take a moment to consider the help God is offering:

Bring the difficulties to God.

—Exodus 18:19

When all things seem against us, to drive us to despair,
We know one gate is open,
One ear will hear our prayer.
There is a praying in detail to be done.
—J. Oswald Sanders

Never forget the nearness of your Lord. Don't worry over
anything whatever; tell God every detail.
—Philippians 4:5–6 (ph)

*Our God is a God who not merely restores, but takes up
our mistakes and follies into His plan for us and brings
good out of them. This is part of the wonder of His gracious
sovereignty.*[7]

—J. I. Packer

*Groanings which cannot be uttered are often prayers that
cannot be refused.*

—Charles H. Spurgeon

59

Overcoming Evil with Good

Just now, focus on your own heart's condition before God:

Lord, help me to . . .
    Rejoice in hope.
    Be patient in tribulation.
    Be steadfast in prayer.
    Let me not be overcome by evil, but let me
    overcome evil with good.
    In Jesus' name. Amen.

(Adapted from Romans 12:12, 21.)

60

Worry

My wife, Katrina, seldom worries. During the time when our daughter was away from God, she occasionally grew angry at our circumstances, and sometimes seemed mystified by my despair. However, she wasn't afflicted with anxiety over our prodigal. That was all right; I had enough anxiety for both of us. Because of it, I began collecting insights on worry:

> *Worry is a small trickle of fear that meanders through the mind until it cuts a channel into which all other thoughts are drained.*
>
> —Anonymous

> *Worry is a destructive process of occupying the mind with thoughts contrary to God's love and care.*
>
> —Norman Vincent Peale

> *Worry is putting question marks where God has put periods.*
>
> —John R. Rice

Worry is the interest we pay on tomorrow's troubles.
—E. Stanley Jones

Worry often gives a small thing a big shadow.
—Anonymous

Worry is a form of atheism, for it betrays a lack of faith and trust in God.
—Bishop Fulton J. Sheen

I would no more worry than I would curse or swear.
—John Wesley

True patience is waiting without worrying.
—Anonymous

Why are you fearful, O you of little faith?
—Matthew 8:26

Do not worry about your life. . . . Which of you by worrying can add one cubit to his stature? So why do you worry . . . ? Therefore do not worry. . . . Do not worry about tomorrow.
—Matthew 6:25, 27–28, 31, 34

Don't worry about anything; instead, pray about everything.
—Philippians 4:6

Gideon built an altar for worshiping the Lord and called it "The Lord Calms Our Fears."
—Judges 6:24 (CEV)

Casting the whole of your care [all your anxieties, all your worries, all your concerns, once and for all] on Him, for He cares for you.
—1 Peter 5:7 (AMP)

61

In Me Too

Right now, God is working in your heart. What do you see Him changing in you?

Lord,
You've told me untold times,
to let You work, to trust Your might.
But my fearful, fretting heart
just will not trust, still walks by sight.
The worries come in crashing waves;
they warp my brain and wreck my soul;
they tempest-toss me through the night.

I'm ashamed, Lord,
for acting like the spying few,
comparing myself to giants
instead of likening giants to You.

Lord, Intervene!
Lord, Overrule!
Not just in my child,
but in me, too.

62

The Lord's Prayer for My Child

Jesus gave the beloved Lord's Prayer as a model, for He prefaced it with the words, "In this manner, therefore, pray" (Matthew 6:9–13). According to Luke 11:1–2, He also used this prayer to answer the disciples' request, "Lord, teach us to pray."

When we adapt the Lord's own model prayer for our deepest need it brings healing to our hearts.

> *Our Father in heaven,*
>> *How holy is Your name!*
>> *May Your kingdom come. May Your will be done in* _____*'s life, even as it is done in heaven.*
>> *Give him this day what he really needs.*
>> *And forgive his sins, helping him to forgive those who sin against him.*
>> *Lead him not into temptation, but deliver him from evil, and from the evil one.*
>> *For Yours is the kingdom, and the power, and the glory forever. Amen.*

63

More Precious than Gold

It was our silver wedding anniversary—August 28, 2001—and, as it happened, the part of the day that we spent with our child turned out to be a little volatile. I felt deeply troubled. A friend detected my dejection from the tone of my e-mail note to him, and this is what he wrote back:

> *Relax and let me do the praying. I'll carry the load today.*
> *Remember that this is your anniversary—August 28. On the*
> *calendar, that is 8/28, as in Romans 8:28. God has promised*
> *that everything that happens today will work for good. Now,*
> *I'll take up the praying, and you enjoy the day with your*
> *wife.*

Such friends are more valuable than our daily bread and more precious than gold and silver.

64

Reveal to Him

I've found the prayers of another to be medicine for my own heart. I don't think the Lord accuses us of plagiarism if we find it appropriate to adapt for our own needs a prayer we find in our studies or worship.

Alan Redpath was a powerful British expositional preacher, pastor for many years of Edinburgh's Charlotte Road Chapel and of Moody Memorial Church of Chicago. Here's my revision of a prayer found in his book, *Getting to Know the Will of God*:

> *Living, loving Lord . . .*
>
> *Reveal to my child the sinfulness of sin and the futility of seeking guidance unless he offers a surrendered heart.*
>
> *Bring him, dear Lord, to Your feet.*
>
> *Draw him to look into Your face and, counting upon Your power, to walk in obedience in the way of peace.*
>
> *In Jesus' name. Amen.[18]*

Research shows that at least 85 percent of all prodigals, including the angriest rebels, eventually return to the faith.

And, as more information becomes available through continuing study, it will almost certainly show that the percentage of prodigals who return is even higher. . . . Evangelical churches are full of returned prodigals.
  —TOM BISSET, *GOOD NEWS ABOUT PRODIGALS*[19]

65

Heal Us Both

Guilt and tormented thoughts can lead to prayer for healing, as this section from my journal confirms:

*I had a relapse of anxiety last night and slept fitfully.
Didn't sleep, really . . . caught in a downward spiral of
guilt and hopelessness. I'm just going further down, deeper,
into blacker water, into despair.*

*Somehow I know this is all my fault; I've failed at the
only thing that I really wanted to do right. Nothing else
matters except the one thing I've messed up.*

*My imagination, which helps me as a writer, I think,
now torments me as a dad. I visualize my child in
situations I never before imagined. How did I let this
happen?*

*Dear Lord, I do not ask to be released from a healthy,
Christlike burden to pray for this child, and I do not ask
for a lifting of godly concern. But this unhealthy, unholy,
unbearable fear, this grief that makes me want to die, this*

intense panic and pain—these, O Lord, are crushing me, and I can't control them.

I'm more of a prodigal than my child, Lord, so please heal us both today. Please break through, lift us up, set us free.

66

The Healing Power of Answered Prayer

Prayer is a balm for the wounded soul, especially when offered with the assurances God gives to those who pray obediently in faith and with perseverance.

Jesus said, "Whatever you ask in My name, that I will do, that the Father may be glorified in the Son. If you ask anything in My name, I will do it" (John 14:13–14).

John explained, "Now this is the confidence that we have in Him, that if we ask anything according to His will, He hears us. And if we know that He hears us, whatever we ask, we know that we have the petitions that we have asked of Him" (1 John 5:14–15).

I've always felt there was a special power in praying for prodigals, for Peter tells us, "The Lord is . . . not willing that any should perish but that all should come to repentance" (2 Peter 3:9).

Years ago I received a letter from a friend named Henry Kastell. He wrote, "I recently got some great news. My sister, Diana, from Phoenix, Arizona, gave up drinking, joined AA, and got saved. She now has a relationship with Christ. . . . All this after years of pain using alcohol. I had prayed for her for years and had almost given up hope; however, that apparently would have been foolish of me. God takes care of things according to *His* will and timetable, which of course are perfect anyway. At any rate, I praise Him for delivering my sister from bondage. God continues to be so good."[20]

One of the most encouraging things I've ever read about prayer is this quote from George Mueller: "The great point is never to give up until the answer comes. I have been praying for sixty-three years and eight months for one man's conversion. He is not converted yet, but he will be! How can it be otherwise? There is the unchanging promise of Jehovah, and on that I rest."

It was later reported that the friend in question was converted at Mueller's funeral.

Jesus' words are appropriate encouragement for us here: We "always ought to pray and not lose heart" (Luke 18:1), and "If you abide in Me, and My words abide in you, you will ask what you desire, and it shall be done for you" (John 15:7).

67

How Can We Keep Going?

One of my challenges during these years has been keeping myself inwardly healthy in order to pastor a church. Our lives or ministries cannot often be suspended for personal crises, at least not for long. We must plod on, working through the pain, and tending to our responsibilities even when our own hearts feel numb with anguish. And we must do it without bleeding too much on others, and sometimes without letting too many people into the hurting places of our hearts.

During that same time, Katrina's multiple sclerosis worsened, and our financial needs hit record peaks; after all, we had three kids in college.

It sounds melodramatic (even to me), but at certain moments I prayed earnestly for the Lord to take me to heaven. It felt as though someone had punched me in the stomach, and I found myself moping around, listless and benumbed, letting my entire ministry be colored by the current crises.

At times, I trudged through the day too emotionally paralyzed to focus my thoughts. Everything I said or did came from the sole perspective of an anguished heart. Returning phone calls, reading books, attending meetings, and giving counsel felt like impossible tasks, to say nothing of preparing and delivering sermons.

When Bill Clinton's White House was engulfed in its infamous sex scandal, reporters expressed amazement at the president's ability to compartmentalize his life, to set the crisis on one burner while he focused his energies elsewhere. I tried that, but couldn't do it. Nor could I successfully mask my feelings or exhibit a countenance at variance with my heart's pain. Yet I had a calling to keep, a job to do, and a church to lead.

Well, my plight is nothing new. David wrote some of his grandest psalms when in the severest pain. Paul was at his bravest when stranded on a storm-tossed ship with little hope of survival. Joseph and Mary's deepest crisis produced the world's greatest hope. Ezekiel's wife died just when he needed her most, and we all know of the trials of godly Job, Daniel in the den of lions, and the three Hebrew children in the furnace.

The Lord, intending us to be "more than conquerors" (Romans 8:37), provides a spiritual arsenal for our benefit. Here are those things that helped me most during the darkest days.

Journaling

I've kept a journal since college days, and over the past several years I've written hundreds of pages describing my anguish, recording my prayers, and listing the Scripture passages God has given me. I routinely record my morning devotions in my journal, but I find it especially useful late at night when I feel too tired to pray and too worried to sleep. I write out my feelings, often as a letter to God, and inscribe by hand the verses He gives me to keep me through the night. For me, making this record has been a tangible way to come into God's presence and to hide myself in the shadow of the Almighty.

Writing a Personal Book

I also have found inestimable help by writing this book, which originally I intended for my eyes only. I wrote it for myself and called it *Prayers and Promises for a Troubled Parent (Me!)*. I read through the entire Bible, listing Scripture passages I converted into prayers for my child. I wrote out hymns, the words of which were easily changed into prayers. I recounted for myself the stories of other parents whose prodigal children have returned to the Lord in answer to earnest prayer. I chronicled some of the great lessons God has taught me through my experiences. And I listed the promises God has given me from His Word. I return to this book nearly every day to remind God—and myself—of the prayers and promises He has shown me. You might want to write your own book of prayers and promises.

Prayer Partners,

I thank God for the "Aarons and Hurs" He has given me as prayer partners. My mother was my most faithful prayer partner, and even now I believe her prayers, prayed in advance, remain at work. And there have been others. Just last week, a friend asked for personal prayer requests for his singles' group to remember during their weekly Bible study. I indirectly alluded to my heart's burden, and he picked up on it, writing back to assure me he would personally devote himself to confidential prayer if I wanted to share more information. I did, and throughout that week his e-mails and prayers were invaluable.

Books

The Lord has also ministered to my soul through several books. How thankful I am for Ruth Bell Graham's *Prodigals and Those Who Love*

Them and that classic *The Kneeling Christian.* Amy Carmichael's *Edges of His Ways* has also been a daily companion. Just last week after a fitful night I opened to this sentence: "It seems to me that we are often called to live a double life: in much tribulation (when we think of the poor world); and yet, in the deepest places of our souls, abundantly satisfied." A fourth book I've kept at hand is *Behind the Ranges* by Geraldine (Mrs. Howard) Taylor, the life-changing story of James O. Fraser. Fraser, a missionary to the Lisu peoples of China, saw remarkable spiritual breakthroughs occur in his work through earnest, protracted prayer. Its applications to me seemed clear.

Patient Coworkers

God has given me a supportive staff with whom I stay perfectly honest regarding my struggles. When things were at the worst, they covered for me, comforted me, prayed for me, and, at times, admonished me.

Exercise

A psychologist friend talked with me at length one day, and insisted that I continue my exercise routine. I had no energy for exercise; my depression had drained all my reserves. "Exercise will release the tension from your body and the endorphins in your body," he said. "Both are essential if you're to get through this." Another friend has since called every day to make sure my exercise time appears on the next day's schedule. Often, when I don't feel I can possibly run or work out, I do it anyway. Afterward, I find my energy and mood elevated, at least a little.

My Spouse

Katrina, despite her crippling MS, has been a tower of strength to me. She doesn't worry as much as I do. She has ample faith that God will bring our child through these years in His own time. Sometimes we weep together, and we often pray together several times a day. Her confidence and faith exceed mine. "I don't know what's wrong with you!" she sometimes says when I want to curl into a fetal position and die. "You act as though God can't deal with this. He loves our child more than you do, and she's going to be fine. She's a jewel, and we've committed her to Him every day of her life. He'll bring her through. It'd be so much better if you'd just trust Him!"

God's Word

The old hymn, "My Faith Has Found a Resting Place" (1891), says, "My heart is leaning on the Word, the Written Word of God." For the past four years, I've leaned on God's Word as never before and I've found light there for even the darkest days. Even as I write this, I'm thinking of last night. My daughter is away for the weekend, and I don't feel at all good about her trip. Last night, my imagination might have wrecked my sleep, but the Lord gave me three thoughts from John 14: "Let not your heart be troubled; trust in Me; and whatever you ask in My name, I will do." Whenever I'd awaken, I would hear Him, as it were, speaking those words to me, and I was then able to sleep.

I've learned so much through the process of working through the elements of emotional struggle and have gradually come to a greater degree of peace, one anchored on the sovereign faithfulness of a caring God who does all things well, and who intends to do a sanctifying work, not only in my child, but in me."

68

Prayer Therapy

R eading books on prayer has become one of my most therapeutic practices. We must be cautious, of course, for it's perilously easy to read about prayer, study prayer, talk about prayer, and collect sayings on prayer, without actually praying. I often find it far easier to spend an hour preparing a sermon on prayer than to spend an hour praying. That said, however, my prayer life and my faith have been strengthened by the insights of others on this subject. Here are some of my favorites:

> *Our loved ones may spurn our appeals, reject our message, oppose our arguments, despise our persons, but they are helpless against our prayers.*
>
> —ADAPTED FROM J. SIDLOW BAXTER

> *Move men, through God, by prayer alone.*
>
> —HUDSON TAYLOR

> *Come on them from above! . . . By intercessory prayer we can hold off Satan from other lives and give the Holy Ghost*

a chance with them. No wonder Jesus put such tremendous emphasis on prayer!

—OSWALD CHAMBERS

They may not listen to us when we plead with them, but they can not hold out if we pray for them. . . . Tell God, and then trust God.

—*The Kneeling Christian*

I never prayed sincerely for anything but it came, at some time . . . somehow, in some shape.

—ADONIRAM JUDSON,
THE UNITED STATES' FIRST MISSIONARY

I must talk to Father about this.

—BILLY BRAY

A day hemmed in prayer is less likely to come unraveled.

—AUTHOR UNKNOWN

69

Prayers from the Benedictions of Scripture

The word *benediction* comes from the Latin words *bene* (well) and *dicere* (to say). It literally means *to speak well* or *to bless*. A benediction is a short blessing that pronounces healing, health, and happiness from God.

The Bible is full of benedictions that can heal your heart. When applied to your child in prayer, they become supplications that God can answer with help and hope.

> *Lord, bless _____ and keep him. Make Your face shine upon my child, and be gracious to him; lift up Your countenance upon him, and give him peace.*
>
> (Adapted from Numbers 6:24–26.)

> *God of peace, who through the blood of the eternal covenant brought back from the dead our Lord Jesus, that great Shepherd of the sheep, may You equip _____ with everything good for doing Your will. Please work in him*

*what is pleasing to You, through Jesus Christ, to whom be
glory for ever and ever. Amen.*

(Adapted from Hebrews 13:20–21, NIV.)

*May the grace of the Lord Jesus Christ, and the love of God,
and the communion of the Holy Spirit be with my child.
Amen.*

(Adapted from 2 Corinthians 13:14.)

*To him who is able to keep my child from falling and to
present him before his glorious presence without fault and
with great joy—to the only God our Savior be glory,
majesty, power, and authority, through Jesus Christ our
Lord, before all ages, now and forevermore! Amen.*

(Adapted from Jude 24–25, NIV.)

70

Words Badly Needed

Today, while feeling especially heavy, I picked up Dr. Paul D. Meier's *Christian Child-Rearing and Personality Development.* I hesitated to open it, fearing I would find lots of things that I had done wrong as a parent. Instead, I found a word of encouragement at both the beginning and at the ending of the book, one that reinforces the truth of Proverbs 22:6: "Train up a child in the way he should go, and when he is old he will not depart from it."

Dr. Meier stresses the importance of a child's early years, saying in his preface: "It is my firm belief that approximately 85 percent of one's adult personality is formed by the time he is six years old. Those first six years, therefore, are obviously the most critical."[22]

I recalled how my wife, Katrina, and I sought to provide our children with love, nurturing, and the truth of the Lord during those early years.

At the very end of Meier's book, I found some words I badly needed:

I sometimes recommend that teenagers who have graduated from high school go several hundred miles away—out of the nest—to develop their God-given talents (preferably but not necessarily at a Christian college), and learn the hard lessons of life by making the necessary mistakes—and then correcting them. If the parents reared the child by God's standards during those crucial first six years of life, when about 85 percent of his personality was formed, he'll do just fine. Trust him. And if the parents haven't reared their child by God's principles, most attempts to teach an eighteen-year-old something he should have learned when he was three years old will be utterly futile. Let him move out to learn from life's hard knocks, and pray that God will mature him.[23]

71

Prayers and Promises
from the Prophet Habakkuk

E ver read the Bible book of Habakkuk? It's short but potent, and
very fitting for those who have a prodigal.

The words of Habakkuk are nothing more than a private conversation between a bewildered prophet (in our case, parent) and his
God. You might want to pause now to read through its three chapters, then reenact it as your own conversation with God. My version
follows:

> *O Lord, how long shall I cry, and You will not hear?*
> *Why do You cause me to see trouble?*
> *Are You not from everlasting,*
> *O Lord my God, my Holy One?*
> *O Lord, revive Your work in the midst of my child!*

> *"Look! Be utterly astounded!*
> *For I will work a work in your days*
> *which you would not believe, though it were told you. . . .*
> *Though it tarries, wait for it; because it shall surely come. . . .*
> *The just shall live by his faith."*

The Lord God is my strength.
He will make my feet like deer's feet;
he will make me walk on the heights.

72

A Parent's Prayer for Wisdom

Be still and listen as you ask God to speak wisdom to your heart:

Lord, grant me the ability to count it all joy as I face these various trials, knowing that the testing of my faith produces patience. May my perseverance increase; may my patience grow to maturity.

Lord, grant me moment-by-moment wisdom. I ask in faith, knowing that every good and perfect gift comes from You, the Father of lights, with whom there is no shadow of turning.

Help me, then, to be swift to listen to my child, slow to speak, and slow to become angry. Remind me that my wrath will not produce Your righteousness.

I ask for both myself and my child that we would lay aside all filthiness of heart and receive with meekness the implanted word which is able to save our souls. Amen.

(Adapted from James 1.)

73

A Helpful Exercise

Sometimes we shy away from Psalm 119 because of its length and repetitive nature. But I challenge you to work your way through this 176-verse segment of Scripture, looking for prayers to pray for yourself or for your prodigal. It is a most helpful exercise, for each of those 176 verses can become a prayer able to bring revival to our children and rest to our souls.

> *Lord, I rise before the dawning of the morning and cry for help. My eyes are awake through the night. Please deal bountifully with _____, that he may live and keep Your word. Open his eyes that he may see wondrous things from Your law. Give him understanding to learn Your commands. Direct his steps by Your word; let no iniquity have dominion over him.*
>
> *He has gone astray like a lost sheep. Seek him, Lord. Make him walk in the path of Your commandments. Incline his heart to Your testimonies, and not to covetousness. Turn away his eyes from worthless things and revive him in Your*

way. Revive him in Your righteousness. Revive him according to Your word.

May he seek You with his whole heart. Oh, let him not wander from Your commandments! May Your word be a lamp to his feet and a light to his path. May he cleanse his way by taking heed to Your word. Help him think about his ways, and turn his feet to Your testimonies.

It is time for You to act, O Lord.

(Adapted from Psalm 119:147–148,17–18, 73,133,176,35–37,40,25,10,105,9,59,126.)

74

The Fourth Watch

Behold, He who keeps Israel [and my child]
Shall neither slumber nor sleep.
—Psalm 121:4

Even a single verse of Scripture can inspire me to poetic prayer:

I used to love the nights, dear Lord,
the fading of the evening lights,
the quiet routine;
the bedtime prayers;
a tale or two; then nodding heads,
three weary kids in cozy beds;
the silent hours of healing rest.
I loved the evenings best.

I hate the evenings now, dear Lord.
My child alone, out in the night,
dives and dens and worthless ends,
flashing lights, unworthy friends,

an empty heart, a search for love,
when all he needs is found above.

I'm going to trust You through this night,
I'm going to walk by faith, not sight.
You slumber not, nor do You sleep,
Your wakeful eye can always keep
my children in Your care.

To Him who tucks me into bed:
Please station angels around his head,
and guard my child wherever he be,
and bring him back, dear Lord, to Thee.

75

Turn Him, Lord

Prayer can be exhausting. Sometimes, when we have little strength to pray, we must replace the length of our prayers with the strength of our prayers. That is, we must find a strong, concise prayer from Scripture, offer it to the Lord, and rest in His power to act on His prayer-a-phrased Word.

These prayers suit the purpose:

> *Turn him from wrongdoing, Lord, and keep him from pride.*
> *Turn away ungodliness from my child.*
> *Withhold him from sinning against You. Keep him from evil, that he may not cause pain.*
> *Where sin abounds, may grace abound much more. May my child reign in life through Christ Jesus . . . being wise about what is good, and innocent about what is evil.*

> (Adapted from Job 33:17; Romans 11:26; Genesis 20:6; 1 Chronicles 4:10; Romans 5:20,17; 16:19.)

76

The Comfort of Psalm 130

Psalm 130 is perfect for troubled parents and other worriers. It always leaves me strengthened. Embrace it as your own today.

> *Out of the depths I have cried to You, O LORD;*
> *LORD, hear my voice!*
> *Let Your ears be attentive*
> *to the voice of my supplications.*
>
> *If You, LORD, should mark iniquities,*
> *O LORD, who could stand?*
> *But there is forgiveness with You,*
> *That You may be feared.*
>
> *I wait for the LORD, my soul waits,*
> *And in His word I do hope.*
> *My soul waits for the LORD*
> *More than those who watch for the morning—*
> *Yes, more than those who watch for the morning.*
> *O Israel, hope in the LORD;*

> *For with the LORD there is mercy,*
> *And with Him is abundant redemption.*
> *And He shall redeem Israel*
> *From all his iniquities.*

77

He's Able

Is God able? Are you ever plagued by little doubts about God's ability to answer prayer, change lives, perform miracles, and redeem circumstances? Read the following verses—read them aloud—and let them reverberate in your heart:

> The LORD is able.
>
> —2 CHRONICLES 25:9

> Is anything too hard for the LORD?
>
> —GENESIS 18:14

> Ah, Lord GOD! Behold, You have made the heavens and the earth by Your great power and outstretched arm. There is nothing too hard for You.
>
> —JEREMIAH 32:17

> "Behold, I am the LORD, the God of all flesh. Is there anything too hard for Me?"
>
> —JEREMIAH 32:27

And He said, "Abba, Father, all things are possible for You."

—MARK 14:36

I know that You can do everything.

—JOB 42:2

God is able.

—MATTHEW 3:9

"The things which are impossible with men are possible with God."

—LUKE 18:27

Jesus looked at them and said, "With men it is impossible, but not with God; for with God all things are possible."

—MARK 10:27

Jesus said to him, "If you can believe, all things are possible to him who believes."

—MARK 9:23

"Assuredly, I say to you, if you have faith as a mustard seed, you will say to this mountain, 'Move from here to there,' and it will move; and nothing will be impossible for you."

—MATTHEW 17:20

"For with God nothing will be impossible."

—LUKE 1:37

The following quotes will provide much comfort to the hurting soul.

> We mothers must take care of the possible and trust God for the impossible. We are to love, affirm, encourage, teach, listen and care for the physical needs of the family. We cannot convict of sin, create hunger and thirst after God, or convert. These are miracles, and miracles are not in our department.
>
> —Ruth Bell Graham[24]

> When you are facing the impossible, you can count on the God of the impossible.
>
> —Amy Carmichael

> [God] encourages us to ask as freely for the impossible as for the possible, since to Him all difficulties are the same size—less than Himself.
>
> —J. Oswald Sanders

> You cannot bring a burden too heavy for God to lift or a problem too hard for Him to solve or a request too big for Him to answer. God does things no one else can do.
>
> —Michael Guido[25]

78

Lifting Me Higher

Reading today in Romans 5:3–5, I found this: "We also glory in tribulations, knowing that tribulation produces perseverance; and perseverance, character; and character, hope. Now hope does not disappoint, because the love of God has been poured out in our hearts by the Holy Spirit who was given to us."

The Lord surely intends to use this anxious time to sanctify me, to lift me higher, to give me maturity. But I must respond correctly.

Two pictures come to mind: a *whirlpool* and a *whirlwind*. Right now I seem caught in a whirlpool, a cycle of fear that pulls me downward, from uncertainty, to stress, to fear, to anguish, and into a dark vortex of hopelessness. I feel like I'm drowning emotionally.

But Romans 5 indicates that the same circumstances could lift me upward and outward, like a whirlwind—if I would just respond with the faith described in Romans 4: Abraham "did not waver at the promise of God through unbelief, but was strengthened in faith, giving glory to God, and being fully convinced that what He had promised He was also able to perform" (verses 20–21).

Lord, even if You don't immediately calm the storm, please calm me. Let me feel the upward winds of Your grace, lifting upward and outward. I believe; strengthen my faith. And add to my faith perseverance, character, hope, and Your own wise love, poured into my heart by Your Spirit.

In Jesus' name. Amen.

79

A Father's Prayer

I have a friend, Steve Elkins, whose music and Christian publications have blessed millions of people. However, he has worried ceaselessly about his own sons, who are very dear to me, too. We've frequently sought to encourage one another. He wrote this prayer one Sunday morning while I preached, and I'm grateful for his permission to share it here with you.

O gracious Father,
    Our children wander, and we grieve and cry out for
You to place angels 'round about them. Protect them.
Cause them to see Your endless glory. Cause them to know
that You and You alone are the one true God to be sought
and honored.
    By the power of the name of Christ Jesus, we do put
Satan behind us; and we call on the name of the Lord, for
You will save our children. They are beloved in Your sight.
    Father, help us endure. Help us be patient. Help us to
lean. Take away the doubt and discouragement. Relieve the
sense of failure, for we assuredly know who the accuser is.

Guard our hearts and minds in Christ Jesus. And return to us those whom we love, yet bring them first to Yourself.

We love You, Lord, and remember that Your mercies are new every morning. The battle is not ours, but Yours, O Lord, Our eyes are on You.[26]

80

Walking in the Day

Today, focus on your desire to see your child lead a godly life:

Heavenly Father,

Teach _____ to abhor what is evil and to cling to what is good. May he cast off the works of darkness and put on the armor of light. Help him walk properly as in the day . . .

not in revelry and drunkenness,

not in lewdness and lust,

not in strife and envy.

But may he put on the Lord Jesus Christ and make no provision for the flesh, to fulfill its lusts. In Jesus' name. Amen.

(Adapted from Romans 13.)

81

The PTL Weapons

I woke up last night feeling helpless—helpless to help my child or his friends. Then it dawned on me that I had three indomitable weapons—code-named PTL—in my fight with Satan for the souls of my children. Why do we ever feel helpless when God intends us to be hopeful?

Prayer

The *P* stands for *prayer*, which is defined as "an offering up of our desires unto God for things agreeable to His will, in the name of Christ, with confession of our sins, and thankful acknowledgment of His mercies" (*Westminster Shorter Catechism*). Prayer is drawing near to God, into His very presence, coming to His footstool, and pleading with Him for what He alone can do—until He does it. It isn't that we're trying to persuade Him to do what He doesn't choose to do. As Archbishop Trench put it, "We must not conceive of prayer as overcoming God's reluctance, but as laying hold of His highest willingness."

The Kneeling Christian describes two aspects to prayer, and only two: *seeking God's glory* and *obtaining God's grace*. Coming into God's presence without sensing His glory is a waste of both God's time and ours. Prayer is, at its essence, a coming into His glorious court. Prayer's greatest purpose is recognizing our heavenly Father's presence. As we do so, we recognize that His throne is a throne of blessing where we may obtain mercy and find grace to help in this time of need (see Hebrews 4:16).

Time

The *T* stands for *time*. It took awhile for the young prodigal in Luke 15 to come to his senses about where he belonged. Maturity, recovery, and rehabilitation are *processes*—and time is on our side, for our times remain in the hands of Jehovah-M'Kaddesh, the "God who sanctifies" (Leviticus 20:8). Think of how long it has taken the Lord to work on you and me. "Please be patient," it's commonly said, "God isn't finished with me yet."

For my child, I'm claiming the promise of Philippians 1:6: "being confident of this very thing, that He who has begun a good work in you will complete it until the day of Jesus Christ."

We find both wisdom and maturity in learning to tell time on God's clock, in developing a sense of His timing, in knowing when to work and when to wait, when to move and when to tarry. While we may not mind the working and moving, we chafe at the waiting and tarrying—but those are elements of faith that God values very highly.

Love

We may not think of *love* as a weapon, but it sends a radioactive blanket over its target. There is no known antidote. Paul said, "Love never fails" (1 Corinthians 13:8), and I've claimed that promise for my child. Love simply means that I'm going to do what's best for my child regardless of whether it seems best for me. It is putting the needs of my child ahead of my own desires. Sometimes that means exercising "tough love," perhaps even telling my child he can't continue to live in our house if he's going to persist in a way of life that consistently disrupts our home. That's exceedingly painful for a parent, yet those might be the wisest and most helpful words we ever speak to our child.

Angry words and demeaning comments or name calling, however, must stop—at least on our part. Remember that love is kind and does not behave rudely; it always seeks the best for the other person. It can be firm and forthright, but it never tears down those to whom it's directed.

According to verse 7, "Love never gives up, never loses faith, is always hopeful, and endures through every circumstance" (NLT).

So, if you wake in the middle of the night feeling helpless, just remind yourself that you have an arsenal of weapons: *prayer, time,* and *love.* These weapons have broken down many a stronghold and reclaimed many a life. These are the weapons God has put at your disposal. You're not powerless after all.

PTL—Praise the Lord!

82

A Strategic Attitude

Hope is a learned trait. Our natural reaction in times of disappointment and crisis is to grow discouraged and pessimistic. For a melancholic like me, reversing emotional gears and developing a positive attitude takes real effort. I can't do it merely by thinking happy thoughts or recalling uplifting platitudes. I can't just hope for the best in a vague sort of way. I can sustain optimism only by burrowing into the Scriptures, trusting the Prince of promises, and choosing to believe in what He tells me in His Word.

I'd like you to meet five other people who took the same approach.

A Psalmist

> *Why are you cast down, O my soul?*
> *And why are you disquieted within me?*
> *Hope in God, for I shall yet praise Him*
> *For the help of His countenance.*
> —Psalm 42:5

An Evangelist

Ruth and I found out that for us, worrying and praying were not mutually exclusive. We trusted the Lord to bring the children through somehow in His own way in due time. . . . Through it all, God did not let us lose hope.

—BILLY GRAHAM,
ABOUT HIS YEARS OF PARENTING PRODIGALS[27]

A Psychologist

Optimism takes the most hopeful view of matters and expects the best outcome in any circumstances. While the prodigal is busy moving from one misadventure to another, optimism will help the parents discipline themselves to see beyond the mess into the aspirations of the child and focus on those. The prodigal does not necessarily want to be identified with his messes or have his nose rubbed in them. The wise mom and dad look to what the prodigal hopes to accomplish.

—S. RUTHERFORD McDILL, JR.[28]

A Pastor

When you say a situation or a person is hopeless, you are slamming the door in the face of God.

—CHARLES L. ALLEN

An Apostle

May the God of hope fill you with all joy and peace as you trust in him, so that you may overflow with hope by the power of the Holy Spirit.

—PAUL (ROMANS 15:13, NIV)

83

A Saturday Night Prayer

One Saturday night, on the last day of March, as I tried to ward off worry long enough to prepare the next day's sermon, the following words came to mind as a prayer for my child. I jotted them in the flyleaf of my Bible and have been offering them as a prayer ever since.

Lord,
Remember_____
Reclaim him from Satan.
Restrain him from evil.
Rebuke errant patterns in his life.
Rectify any careless ways.
Rekindle his spiritual fervor and revive his soul.
Reassure him of Your plan for him.
Reinforce his faith.
Release Your Spirit into his heart and
Recruit him for Your kingdom's work.
In Jesus' name. Amen.

84

Leaving Him in God's Hands

The psalms are heart cries—sometimes of praise, sometimes of pain, sometimes of prayer, sometimes of pondering. But, somehow, the psalms always give us hope. Offer the following prayer, modeled after various verses in the Psalms, for your prodigal, and leave him in God's all-capable hands tonight.

Lord, prepare _____'s heart, and cause Your ear to hear. Lead him, O Lord, in Your righteousness. Make his way straight before Your face. Show him Your ways, O Lord; teach him Your paths. Lead him in Your truth and teach him. Keep his soul, and deliver him. Teach him Your way, O Lord, and lead him. For Your name's sake, lead him and guide him. Pull him out of the net secretly laid for him. Instruct him and teach him in the way he should go. Guide him with Your eye. May he not be like the horse or mule, which have no understanding, which must be harnessed with bit and bridle.

Lead him in the paths of righteousness for Your name's

sake, for into Your hand I commit my child, O Lord God of truth. Let Your mercy, O Lord, be upon us, just as we hope in You.

(Adapted from Psalms 10:17; 5:8; 25:4–5,20; 27:11; 31:3–4; 32:8–9; 23:3; 31:5; 33:22.)

85

A Hopeful Letter

A woman who grew up on the mission field wrote me a letter:

I began experimenting with sexual activity as a senior in high school. My junior year in college I got pregnant and wasn't exactly sure who the father was. I chose to have an abortion, which Satan used to keep me even more tightly bound.

My parents were still serving overseas and were not aware of any of this. Through conversations with church friends, they knew I wasn't very active in church, but I managed to keep everything else from them. This in itself was agony. But I finally taught my conscience to be quiet, so I could get involved in bigger, more life-threatening choices with decreasing discomfort. In retrospect, I see that God in loving kindness and faithfulness never let me go. He brought me through by His grace alone and through my parents' daily prayers for me.

There was nothing anyone could have said to me; their admonishing only brought deeper guilt and built the wall higher.

[My boyfriend] and I got married a year and a half after we met. Eight and a half months later we had our first child. When she was about six months old, God finally got my attention and made me realize my need for Him and His salvation.

He had been drawing me gently and quietly since [my daughter's] birth. [My husband] and I began attending church regularly because we wanted to be responsible parents. God spoke to me, forgave me, cleansed me, and made me wholly His one morning in my living room when I was all alone.

What an awesome God!

86

None Like You

Right now, consider God's power and His ability to act in your child's life:

O Lord God,

There is none like You in heaven above or on earth below. You are a God of mercy and a keeper of promises. Not even heaven or the heaven of heavens can contain You. Yet You listen to Your servants who pray before You day and night.

Now, please hear in heaven, Your dwelling place, and when You hear, forgive; for there is no one who does not sin.

Send forth Your mercy toward my child. When he experiences famine in his life, pestilence or blight or mildew; when the enemy besieges him; whatever plague or sickness there is, teach him to know the plague of his own heart, to spread out his hands toward You, and to seek Your forgiveness.

Grant him Your compassion. Teach him the good way in which he should walk, and incline his heart to Yourself, to walk in all Your ways and to keep Your commands. Let his heart be loyal to You, the Lord my God, to walk in Your statutes.

May Your eyes be open to the supplication of your servant, and Your ears open to my cry.

(Adapted from Solomon's prayer in 1 Kings 8.)

87

Lord, Preserve

Today, focus on God's work in your child's life during this difficult time:

Father God, You alone are the Lord,
*   You have made the heavens, with all their host, the earth*
and everything on it, the seas and all that is in them, and You
preserve them all. Surely, Lord, You are concerned for our
children, for You have said, "Leave your fatherless children,
I will preserve them alive; and let your widows trust in me."
*   Lord, preserve _____ from trouble and*
surround him with songs of deliverance. Do not withhold
Your mercies from my child, but let Your loving kindness
and Your truth continually preserve him. Preserve him and
keep him alive, and may he be blessed on the earth.
*   Preserve my child from all evil; preserve his soul.*
Preserve his going out and his coming in from this time forth.
Protect and preserve his life; bless him in the land and do not
surrender him to the desire of the enemy. Turn his eyes away
from worthless things and preserve his life according to Your

word. Preserve his life in Your righteousness. Preserve his life according to Your love. Preserve his life according to Your laws. Preserve his life according to Your promise.

Teach him that wisdom and knowledge are pleasant to his soul, that discretion will preserve him, that understanding will keep him, to deliver him from the way of evil, from those who speak perverse things.

Sanctify my child completely; may his whole spirit, soul, and body be preserved blameless at the coming of our Lord Jesus Christ. Deliver him from every evil work and preserve him for Your heavenly kingdom. To You be glory forever and ever. Amen!

(Adapted from Nehemiah 9:6; Jeremiah 49:11; Psalms 32:7;
40:11; 41:2; 121:7–8; 41:2; 119:37,40,88,149,154;
Proverbs 2:10–12; 1 Thessalonians 5:23; 2 Timothy 4:18.)

In this context, *preserve* means to keep safe from injury, harm, or destruction; to keep alive, intact, or free from decay.

88

Restoring Hope

In 701 B.C., Judea was invaded by Assyrian forces. The forces of King Hezekiah were no match for those of the mighty Assyrian ruler Sennacherib. Hezekiah found himself with fears beyond description and with problems that defied solution, just as we do when our children are in crisis.

This story contains such important lessons that it is repeated three times in the Bible: 2 Kings 18–19; 2 Chronicles 32; and Isaiah 36–37. Take a few minutes now to do a brief Bible study based on this case study. Read one of the accounts, then notice these principles:

- Ask others in whom you have confidence to pray. (See 1 Samuel 12:2,19; Daniel 2:17–18; Matthew 18:19–20.)

- Spread out your problems before the Lord. (See Psalms 88:9; 143:6; Mark 10:46–52; Hebrews 4:16.)

- Realize that God can providentially orchestrate events to accomplish His purposes. (See Genesis 45:5–8;

50:20; Psalm 33:10–11; Proverbs 16:9; 19:21; 20:24; Romans 8:28.)

- Remember that God uses angels to assist us in difficult times. (See Psalms 34:7; 91:11; Matthew 18:10; Acts 5:19; 12:7; 27:23; Hebrews 1:14.)

89

A Halloween Victory

Mary Myers felt too tired to pray and too worried to sleep. Her daughter was in deep trouble. The nights seemed cold and dark; her pain, unending.

Her daughter, Anna, had been causing problems since childhood, but her concerns became crises during her teen years as Anna started smoking, drugging, and skipping school. After high school, a friend lured Anna into Satanism, and she began living in a house with two warlocks and three witches. Anna learned how to channel spirits, cast spells, and ply the darkest waters of the supernatural. Mary brought me into the story then and allows me to share it now.

With a mother's breaking heart, Mary groaned as she heard of Anna, egged on by friends and fiends, biting people, drawing their blood, drinking it. Frantic and desperate, she confronted her daughter as often as she dared, but futilely. On one occasion, Mary narrowly escaped harm as Anna lunged at her, trying to slit her throat with a knife. It was the family dog who intervened, charging at Anna, biting her wrist, and saving Mary from injury.

Finally, Mary asked her friends to join her in earnest, effectual prayer. That's when things began to change. Anna's boyfriend left her, and her other support systems began falling away, leaving her lonely and thoughtful. Mary prayed harder. Anna sunk into depression and began feeling terribly frightened. She felt as though magnetic forces were drawing her, despite her protests, toward God. Mary remained earnest in prayer.

Anna, feeling guilty and dirty, began to grow tired of her lifestyle. Mary pressed her friends to keep praying.

Appropriately, during one Halloween season Anna fell to her knees and begged God to take away her pain. She gave up the sins of her past, renounced the Enemy, and turned in simple faith to Jesus Christ.

Her prodigality was no match for her mom's prayers.

90

Striving in Prayer

Epaphras, who is one of you and a servant of Christ Jesus, sends greetings. He is always wrestling in prayer for you, that you may stand firm in all the will of God, mature and fully assured.

—Colossians 4:12 (NIV)

Epaphras is a role model for parents in our prayerful concern for our children. Notice these things about him:

Why He Prayed

According to Colossians 1:6–8, his efforts resulted in the birth of the church of Colosse. Then his spiritual children faced the dangers of heresy (2:4). Imprisoned with Paul, Epaphras could do nothing but pray.

How He Prayed

Two words in Colossians 4:12 describe Epaphras's prayers:

> *Always: He was continually wrestling in prayer for them.*
> *Ardently: He was always wrestling in prayer for them.*
> *The word wrestling is a translation of the Greek word*
> *agonizomai, source of our English term agony. The root*
> *agon has reference to both athletic contests and military*
> *combat and echoes the word used of Jesus in Gethsemane:*
> *"Being in agony, He prayed more earnestly" (Luke 22:44).*
>
> *I can imagine [Epaphras] rising from his knees utterly spent,*
> *completely exhausted.*
>
> —Guy King

> *The picture is of a perspiring wrestler straining every muscle,*
> *summoning every last ounce of strength as he contends in the*
> *games. Epaphras prayed to the point of exhaustion.*
>
> —J. Oswald Sanders

> *Real prayer is exhausting.*
>
> —Anonymous

What He Prayed

His prayer is given in Colossians 4:12 (niv): "that you may stand firm in all the will of God, mature and fully assured." Adopt this prayer as your own today:

> *Lord, I am wrestling in prayer for my child, that he may*
> *stand firm in all Your will, mature and fully assured.*

91

Sic Him

Here's a prayer I composed one day based on the title of the famous poem "The Hound of Heaven" by Francis Thompson.

Sic him, Hound of Heaven;
Sniff out his trail, pursue!
Nip at his heels both day and night.
His stubborn will subdue.
His deadened heart renew.

Chase him, Hound of Heaven;
Breathe down his neck, convict!
Restrain his soul from sinfulness.
His waywardness restrict.
His demon-guests evict.

Catch him, Hound of Heaven;
Though You must growl and bite!
Endue his soul with self-control,
Come win this terrible fight.
And give him spiritual sight.

92

Fasting

Occasionally, during bleak periods, I would utterly lose appetite, too distraught to think of food or even feel hunger. Granted, we must guard against the cycle of worry: loss of appetite, undernourishment, physical weakness, and emotional and spiritual collapse. At the same time, during such seasons I have found it helpful to fast, devoting extra time to prayer, particularly during usual mealtimes. On other occasions, even when not robbed of appetite, I still skipped meals in order to pray and fast for my child. I finally developed a consistent pattern of fasting every Wednesday.

Thousands of articles and books have been written about fasting, but to me, J. Oswald Sanders sums it up best with his usual insightfulness:

> *While fasting is always optional in the New Testament, the record indicates that it was resorted to in the face of special temptation (Matt. 4:2); where there was a yearning after a closer walk with God (1 Cor. 7:5); where there was deep concern for evangelizing the regions beyond (Acts 13:1–3); where there was spiritual travail for the development of a*

church (Acts 14:21–23); where some stubborn situation had yielded to no other method (Matt. 17:21). There is still a place for prayer and fasting, though not on legalistic grounds.[29]

The stubborn situation Sanders cited from Matthew 17 has specific reference to a father's battling invisible hosts for the welfare of his son.

Fasting is a versatile discipline that can be practiced in different ways. Perhaps the Lord will impress you with a system or strategy of personal fasting that will aid your spiritual strength and help win the victory.

93

Growing Up in All Things

Today, focus on your desire to see your child follow God:

Dear Lord, I ask that _____ might walk worthy of the calling with which he was called—no longer a child tossed to and fro or walking as the pagans do. But may he grow up in all things unto Him who is the Head—even Christ.

May he give no place to the Devil, nor may any corrupt word proceed from his mouth, but only what is necessary for edification, that it may impart grace to the hearers. Keep him, Lord, from grieving Your Holy Spirit.

Empower _____ to avoid fornication and all uncleanness and covetousness.

Restrain him from being drunk with alcohol; enable him to be filled with the Spirit.

I now take up the shield of faith with which I can quench all the fiery darts of the enemy, and I dedicate myself to praying always in the Spirit for my child, with all perseverance and supplication.

(Adapted from Ephesians 4–6.)

94

The Battle Is the Lord's

As you read these words, rest in the Lord's power to fight this battle:

> *My brethren, be strong in the Lord and in the power of His might. . . . Today you are on the verge of battle with your enemies. Do not let your heart be faint, do not be afraid, and do not tremble or be terrified because of them; for the Lord your God is He who goes with you, to fight for you against your enemies.*
>
> *Do not be afraid nor dismayed because of this great multitude, for the battle is not yours, but God's. You will not need to fight in this battle. Position yourselves, stand still and see the salvation of the Lord . . . !*
>
> *You must not fear . . . for the Lord your God Himself fights for you. You will not need to fight in this battle.*
>
> *The Lord is a man of war; the Lord is His name. With our enemy is an arm of flesh; but with us is the Lord our God, to help us and to fight our battles. Who is this King of glory? The Lord strong and mighty, the Lord mighty in battle.*

We are more than conquerors through Him who loved us.

We are of God, little children, and have overcome them, because He who is in you is greater than he who is in the world. And this is the victory that has overcome the world— our faith.

"Not by might nor by power, but by My Spirit," says the Lord of hosts.

(Adapted from Ephesians 6:10; Deuteronomy 20:3–4; 2 Chronicles 20:15,17; Deuteronomy 3:22; Exodus 15:3; 2 Chronicles 32:8; Psalm 24:8; Romans 8:37; 1 John 4:4; 5:4; Zechariah 4:6.)

95

Battling Anxiety

Paul's words in Philippians 4 provide God's six-point formula for overcoming worry:

1. Rejoice in the Lord (v.4)

When in verse 4 Paul says, "Rejoice in the Lord," he is not coining a new phrase but simply quoting an Old Testament command. The primary Hebrew root for *rejoice* means to shine, to be bright. This phrase could be translated, "Brighten up in the Lord! Put on a happier face. Lift your countenance."

2. Be as Gentle as Possible in These Relationships (v.5)

Much damage occurs when we speak quickly or react in anger. It's important to do our best to keep the lines of communication open.

3. Remember, the Lord Is Near (v.5)

God's presence is closer than you realize. Learn to concentrate on His nearness and to make a practice of remembering His presence. Turn and speak to Him as naturally as to a friend.

4. Don't Worry About Anything (v.6)

"Be anxious for nothing" (verse 6) is not *my* advice; it's God's command. And all His commands are promises in reverse, for He will always enable us, through His Spirit, to obey His commands. But in practical terms, how can we do this while overcome with concern? By proceeding to the next point.

5. Pray About Everything—with Thanksgiving (v.6)

Turn your problems into prayers and your impossibilities into intercessions. Sometimes the darkest days must be lit up with praise before the solution shines forth.

6. Focus on God's True, Noble, Right, Pure, Lovely, Admirable Promises (vv.7–9)

Whatever is positive and hopeful, think on those things. Choose—by sheer willpower, if necessary—to turn the focus of your thoughts onto the Lord. As you concentrate on Him, He'll turn His attention to your burden.

And the promise? Both the God of peace and the peace of God will be yours.

96

Dispersing Poisonous Gas

Among the most encouraging books I've read is *Mountain Rain,* the biography of James O. Fraser, who was a missionary among the Lisu people on the China-Burma border. His labors appeared futile for years, but at last the Holy Spirit swept like a mighty wind over scores of Lisu villages, and hundreds of families came to Christ.

I began to see that the same prayer power that accomplished change for the Lisu can also bring my child back to the Lord.

During his years of faithful intercession and waiting, Fraser penned updated reports to his prayer circle back in England. In one of them, he described Satan's hold over the Lisu in a way that we, as parents, can understand regarding our children.

> *We are not dealing with an enemy that fires at the head only—that keeps the mind only in ignorance—but with an enemy who uses poison gas attacks which wrap the people round with deadly effect, and yet are impalpable, elusive. What would you think of the folly of the soldier who fired a gun into the gas, to kill it or drive it back? Nor would it be of any more avail to teach or preach to the Lisu here, while*

they are held back by these invisible forces. Poisonous gas cannot be dispersed, I suppose, in any other way than by the wind springing up and dispersing it. Man is powerless. But the breath of God can blow away all those miasmic vapors from the atmosphere of a village, in answer to your prayers.[30]

One grand old hymn talks about the power of God's breath. Sing or say it as a heartfelt prayer for your child today.

> *Breathe on* _____ *, Breath of God,*
> *Fill him with life anew,*
> *That he may love what Thou dost love,*
> *And do what Thou wouldst do.*
>
> *Breathe on him, Breath of God,*
> *Until his heart is pure,*
> *Until his will is one with Thine,*
> *To do and to endure.*
>
> *Breathe on him, Breath of God,*
> *Till he is wholly Thine*
> *Until this earthly part of him*
> *Glows with Thy fire divine.* (1878)

97

Ammunition from Isaiah

If you're feeling overwhelmed, try reading Isaiah 40–66. Written to people overwhelmed by life, these words are among the most comforting in Scripture.

Here's a prayer composed from the powerful prophecies of Isaiah:

> *Lord, plant _____'s feet squarely on the highway of*
> *holiness. Teach him Your ways; may he walk in Your paths,*
> *in Your light. May his ears hear a word behind him, saying,*
> *"This is the way, walk in it," whenever he turns to the right*
> *hand or to the left. Make the crooked places in his life*
> *straight and the rough places smooth.*
>
> *O Lord, You have said, "I will pour My Spirit on your*
> *descendants, and My blessings on your offspring." You have*
> *said, "I will save your children." Please do these things for*
> *my child, and do not forsake him. For Your hand is not*
> *shortened that it cannot save.*
>
> (Adapted from Isaiah 35:8; 2:3,5; 30:21;
> 40:4; 44:3; 49:25; 42:16; 50:2.)

98

The Omnipotence of Prayer

Right now, rest in the knowledge of answered prayers:

We can accomplish far more by our prayers than by our work. Prayer is omnipotent; it can do anything God can do! When we pray, God works. All fruitfulness in service is the outcome of prayer—of the worker's prayers, or of those who are holding up holy hands on his behalf.

There is no doubt whatever that the devil opposes our approach to God in prayer, and does all he can to prevent the prayer of faith. His chief way of hindering us is to try to fill our minds with the thought of our needs, so that they shall not be occupied with thoughts of God, our loving Father, to Whom we pray. He wants us to think more of the gift than of the Giver. The Holy Spirit leads us to pray for a brother. We get as far as "O God, bless my brother"—and away go our thoughts to the brother, and his affairs, and his difficulties, his hopes and his fears, and away goes prayer! How hard the devil makes it for us to concentrate our thoughts upon God! This is why we urge people to get a realization of the glory of God, and the power of God, and the presence of God, before offering up any petition.[31]

—AN UNKNOWN CHRISTIAN, IN *THE KNEELING CHRISTIAN*

99

The Beginning of Wisdom

Today, pray about your desire to see your child focus on God:

Lord, sow within _____'s soul a reverent fear of Yourself, for that is the beginning of wisdom. Help him receive Your words, treasure Your commands, and incline his heart toward Your wisdom.

When sinners entice him, help him say, "No!" Keep him from walking in the way with them. Keep his foot from their path.

Give him the wisdom to keep himself from the way of evil, from the man who speaks perverse things, from those who leave the paths of uprightness to walk in the ways of darkness, from those who rejoice in doing evil, from those whose ways are crooked and who are devious, from the immoral.

Help him instead to trust in You with all his heart, leaning not on his own understanding. In all his ways, may he acknowledge You, that You may direct his paths.

(Adapted from Proverbs 1–3.)

100

The Gift of Hymns

For difficult times, God gives us the gift of hymns. The great hymns of the faith—both the classics of English hymnody and the gospel songs of the American era—contain endorphins for the soul. Sometimes when most distressed, I can only sing.

Sometimes I turn hymns into prayers for my children.

Spirit of God, descend upon _____'s heart;
Wean it from earth, through all its pulses move;
Stoop to his weakness, mighty as Thou art,
And make him love Thee as he ought to love. (1854)

Holy Spirit, Light divine
Shine upon this child of mine
Chase the shades of night away,
Turn his darkness into day.

Holy Spirit, all divine
Dwell within this child of mine

Cast down every idol throne
Reign supreme and reign alone. (1864)

Revive him again, fill his heart with Thy love;
May his soul be rekindled with fire from above.
Hallelujah! Thine the glory, Hallelujah! Amen;
Hallelujah! Thine the glory; Revive him again. (1863)

101

God's Magnetism

Do you know the words of Fanny Crosby's old song?

> *I am Thine, O Lord—I have heard Thy voice,*
> *And it told Thy love to me. (1875)*

Commonly called "Draw Me Nearer," this hymn is a wonderful comfort to those suffering anxiety. I found that I could easily convert the chorus into a prayer for my child.

> *Draw _____ nearer, nearer blessed Lord*
> *To the cross where Thou hast died;*
> *Draw him nearer, nearer, nearer blessed Lord*
> *To Thy precious, bleeding side.*

That prompted me to look up the word draw in the Bible, and from that search came the following prayer:

> *Dear Lord,*
> *Jesus said, "I, if I am lifted up from the earth, will draw all peoples to Myself."*

Draw _____ out of many waters, and deliver him from the strong enemy. Draw him to Yourself with loving kindness, with gentle cords, with bands of love. Draw him, and may he run after You, to be glad and rejoice in You.

May he draw near with a true heart in full assurance of faith, having his heart sprinkled from an evil conscience and his body washed with pure water.

Help him realize that it is good for him to draw near to You, to put his trust in the Lord his God, and to declare Your wonderful works.

(Adapted from John 12:32; Psalm 18:16–17;
Jeremiah 31:3; Hosea 11:4; Song of Solomon 1:4;
Hebrews 10:22; Psalm 73:28.)

102

Perfect What Is Lacking

Today, ask God to work in your child's life and thank Him for His faithfulness:

> *I give thanks to You, Lord, for _____, making mention of him always in my prayers, and cherishing him with the love of a nursing mother and an affectionate father.*
>
> *I ask You, therefore, Father, to establish him and encourage him concerning his faith. Keep the tempter away. Perfect what is lacking in his heart. Make him increase and abound in love, and establish his heart blameless in holiness before You, Lord Jesus.*
>
> *May he abstain from sexual immorality, and possess his own body in sanctification and honor, not in passion and lust. Help him to abstain from every form of evil.*
>
> *And may You, the God of peace, sanctify my child completely; may his whole spirit, soul, and body be preserved blameless at the coming of our Lord Jesus Christ.*
>
> *You, O Lord, are faithful.*
>
> *You, O Lord, will do it.*

(Adapted from 1 Thessalonians.)

103

From Sigh to Song

Have you ever noticed how many psalms begin with a sigh and end with a song? That's often the way with our prayers.

Save us, O God! For the waters have come up to our necks. We sink in deep mire, where there is no standing; we have come into deep waters, where the floods overflow us.

Lord, be merciful to _____ and bless him, and cause Your face to shine upon him. Make haste, O God, to deliver him! Make haste to help him, O Lord! Early may he seek You. . . .

Blessed be God, who has not turned away my prayer, nor His mercy from me! I will praise You, the help of my countenance and my God.

(Adapted from Psalms 69:1–2; 67:1; 70:1; 63:1; 66:20; 42:11.)

104

Teach Him Your Way

The psalmist David twice asked God, "Teach me Your way." In Psalm 27:11, he prayed, "Teach me Your way, O Lord, and lead me in a smooth path." And in 86:11, he added, "Teach me Your way, O Lord; I will walk in Your truth."

He but echoed an older prayer, one that Moses prayed in Exodus 33:13: "Teach me your ways so that I may know you and continue to find favor with you" (NIV).

Several years ago, B. Mansell Ramsey, using that same phrase as inspiration, wrote a beautiful hymn. I was delighted at how easily I could convert his words into a prayer for my child:

> *Teach_____Thy way,*
> *O Lord, Teach him Thy way!*
> *Thy guiding grace afford—Teach him Thy way!*
> *Help him to walk aright, More by faith less by sight;*
> *Lead him with heavenly light, Teach him Thy way.*
>
> *When he is sad at heart, Teach him Thy way!*
> *When earthly joys depart, Teach him Thy way!*

In hours of loneliness, In times of dire distress,
In failure or success, Teach him Thy way!

When doubts and fears arise, Teach him Thy way!
When storms o'erspread the skies, Teach him Thy way!
Shine thro' the cloud and rain, Thro' sorrow, toil, and pain,
Make Thou his pathway plain, Teach him Thy way!

Long as his life shall last, Teach him Thy way!
Where'er his lot be cast, Teach him Thy way!
Until the race is run, Until the journey's done,
Until the crown is won, Teach Him Thy way! (1919)

105

Praying with Hymns

Here are two hymns that I adapted into prayers.

> *Come, Thou Almighty King,*
> *Help _____ Thy Name to sing,*
> *Help him to praise.*
> *Father! All glorious, be all victorious,*
> *Come and reign over us, Ancient of Day.*[32]

> *Send a great revival to his soul.*
> *Send a great revival to his soul.*
> *Let the Holy Spirit come and take control;*
> *and send a great revival to his soul.*[33]

Here are two other prayers you can sing to the Lord today:

> *Come, Holy Spirit, heav'nly Dove, with all*
> *Thy quick'ning pow'rs*
> *Kindle a flame of sacred love, within this child of ours.*

Take away his love of sinning,
Alpha and Omega be
End of faith as its beginning,
Set his heart at liberty. (1747)

106

God's Sermon to Me

It took me four years to work through my anguish. I've been a Christian most of my life and have had a daily walk with the Lord for more than thirty years. I've preached thousands of sermons, written hundreds of pieces, and authored more than twenty books. But my faith wasn't adequate for the prodigal's challenge, and I became a basket case: sometimes angry, always anxious, and often deeply depressed.

When people came to me for counseling, I'd compare their problem with mine and spend the rest of the time telling them my story. My sermons became self-help lectures aimed at me. My time with my wife, Katrina, and with our other children was overshadowed by the one not there.

I found myself repeatedly praying the words of the distraught father in Mark 9:24: "Lord, I believe; help my unbelief!" I knew God's peace was a reality, but I couldn't seem to experience it. Yet I did have enough sense to realize that God felt as concerned about me and about my child as I did and that He intended to use this trial to perfect and develop my trust in Him.

Then, approximately four years into the difficulty, several Scripture passages came together in my mind that helped me turn a corner. It was as if these verses had been launched from heaven like laser-guided missiles, and they found their target in my brain. A level of peace finally swept over me and never left. I've typed these verses on a sheet of paper, and I'm looking at them as I write this—page 1 of my devotional notebook.

The first one, Colossians 3:3, had been rolling around in the back of my mind for a few weeks when a dear friend, missionary Tim Keener, arrived one Sunday night to speak at our church. He could tell by my countenance that I was in pitiful shape. We stepped aside and prayed together, then the service began. He based his message that night on the very verse I'd been mulling, Colossians 3:3: "For you died, and your life is hidden with Christ in God."

That, I realized, was the necessary step. I had to "die" to my child. My love for her didn't need to die, but rather my anxiety over her. I had to step away, to leave her at the cross, to detach myself from the crippling emotions that did neither of us any good. I had to stop feeling so responsible. I had to die to all that, and I had to realize that God was all I needed, that I could hide in Him until the storm passed by.

Then, almost immediately, came the second Scripture, Psalm 73:25–26:

> *Whom have I in heaven but You?*
> *And there is none upon earth that I desire besides You.*
> *My flesh and my heart fail;*
> *But God is the strength of my heart and my portion forever.*

It is possible that I loved my child too much? No, but it's possible I loved the Lord too little. Remember how God tested Abraham to see if his love for Isaac had become idolatrous (see Genesis 22)? I thought of Jesus' warning in Matthew 10:37: "He who loves son or daughter more than Me is not worthy of Me." I had to make sure that He alone dominated my heart and mind.

Then two other verses came to mind, rounding out the frame: "When they looked up, they saw no one except Jesus" (Matthew 17:8, NIV) and "They looked to him and were radiant" (Psalm 34:5, NIV).

That, plus the story of Jehoshaphat in 2 Chronicles 20 (which we'll look at in the next devotion), finally broke through thick, long-overcast skies and let in shafts of light after four years of heavy rain and deep gloom.

I'd be delighted if you also wanted to make them your own.

107

Ten Truths

While Psalm 34:5, Psalm 73, Matthew 17, and Colossians 3 broke the chains of worry in my heart, another passage virtually liberated me from the Devil's dungeon: the story of Jehoshaphat in 2 Chronicles 20.

I can't describe how much this passage helps me. As clear as a roadmap, it contains ten truths for handling the predicament of a prodigal child—or any other crisis, for that matter.

King Jehoshaphat was minding his own business, trying to be a good leader for God's people, the nation of Judah, and the land seemed peaceful and quiet. Then, suddenly, a crisis struck from nowhere. A seemingly invincible, multinational army had begun marching toward Jerusalem. Jehoshaphat and his people faced total destruction.

Enter the ten truths.

Truth 1: It's All Right to Be Alarmed—at First

Verse 3 says: "Jehoshaphat was alarmed by this news" (NLT). It's a terrible moment when we're hit by bad news, when the phone rings, when a friend pulls us aside, when the police arrive during the night. Who wouldn't feel alarmed? I'm ashamed to admit that my first reaction to any crisis is hyperventilation—my heart races and I can't get my breath. All of us know that terrible feeling of adrenaline shooting through our veins like a powerful injection. That's a natural reaction, but that isn't where we want to stay for long.

Truth 2: Take the Problem Straight to God

Living in a perpetual state of crisis and fear isn't all right. Notice the rest of verses 3–4: "Jehoshaphat was alarmed by this news and sought the Lord for guidance. He also gave orders that everyone throughout Judah should observe a fast. So people from all the towns of Judah came to Jerusalem to seek the Lord" (NLT). We have to get a grip on ourselves and do the next logical thing—go straight to the Lord with our need.

Truth 3: Pray Earnestly

Verses 5–13 record the prayer that King Jehoshaphat offered before the people. Standing in the center of the temple courtyard with his frightened people around him, he didn't try to soften the news or sugarcoat the problem. He just led the nation in prayer, matter-of-factly acknowledging God's greatness and His past faithfulness to them, and then saying, "O our God, will You not judge them? For we have no power against this great multitude that is coming against us; nor do we know what to do, but our eyes are upon You" (verse 12).

When I read those words, a great burden rolled off my back. I had a vicious enemy coming against me—Satan—trying to defeat me and to destroy someone close to me. For four years I hadn't known exactly what to do. Now I determined to fix my eyes squarely on

God, live or die. While I had worked to do this repeatedly in the past, now somehow by God's grace, this state of mind was taking hold.

Truth 4: Let God Handle It

When Jehoshaphat finished his prayer, no one knew what to do or say next, and the silence felt as thick as fog. But suddenly, a voice cried out. The Holy Spirit descended upon a man named Jahaziel. He became God's microphone, in essence saying, "Thus says the Lord to you: 'Do not be afraid nor be dismayed because of this great multitude, for the battle is not yours, but God's.'"

Has there ever been a message so short and so simple, yet so stupendous? Take that as an inspired promise for you in your situation, whatever it is. Claim it as a word from Him who is able to do exceedingly abundantly beyond anything we can imagine (see Ephesians 3:20).

Truth 5: Cast out Fear

Jahaziel continued in verse 17: "You will not need to fight in this battle. Position yourselves, stand still and see the salvation of the Lord, who is with you, O Judah and Jerusalem! Do not fear or be dismayed; tomorrow go out against them, for the Lord is with you." Twice the Lord commands the people to cast out fear (verses 15, 17), and twice He reminds them that He is there with them, closer than their own troops (verse 17). Remind yourself of all the "fear nots" in the Bible and of the many reassurances God gives that He dwells among and within His people. He'll not leave you nor forsake you. He is near, closer than you think, and closer to your children than you realize.

Right now, affirm His presence. He's with you and with your kids at the same time. Even when we walk through the valley of the shadow, we needn't be afraid, for He is with us (see Psalm 23:4).

Truth 6: Worship During the Night

As the mass prayer meeting ended, the sun sank low and a blanket of darkness descended over the people of Jerusalem—surely the longest night of their lives. The next day they would face an army with vast resources, an army intent on destroying them completely. Their children's lives hung in the balance, and humanly speaking, the odds were stacked against them. They could have worried themselves sick throughout that night of uncertainty and terror, but instead they worshiped. Verse 18 says, "Jehoshaphat bowed his head with his face to the ground, and all Judah and the inhabitants of Jerusalem bowed before the Lord, worshiping the Lord."

Every night when our children are away, we have a choice: we can either worry or worship. I have a friend who hasn't heard from his son in six years, who doesn't know if he's dead or alive. But what an inspiration to see this friend every Sunday standing in church, lifting his eyes to heaven, singing to the Lord, and worshiping.

God intervenes for those who worship Him.

Truth 7: Trust Him

The story continues in verse 20: "So they rose early in the morning and went out into the Wilderness of Tekoa; and as they went out, Jehoshaphat stood and said: 'Hear me, O Judah and all you inhabitants of Jerusalem: Believe in the Lord your God, and you shall be established; believe His prophets, and you shall prosper.'"

Everything comes down to faith. During one difficult month, I read through Matthew's gospel, underlining all the references to faith and belief. It amazed me to discover that Jesus looked at virtually everyone He met, using His X-ray vision, to detect faith or its absence. He expressed amazement when He found it in unexpected places, such as in the Roman centurion of Luke 7. And He felt equally amazed when He didn't find it where He should have, such as in His hometown of Nazareth (see Mark 6:6).

Jesus is gratified when we trust Him despite the circumstances we face; and He is equally dismayed when we don't trust Him despite the assurances He's given.

Find the promises that meet your need, put your name in them, claim them, and choose to trust Him, come what may. "Faith in God," said V. Raymond Edman, "is a quiet confidence that He hears our prayers and answers in His own way and time."

Truth 8: Sing in the Victory

The army went forth into war—or rather, to stand still and watch the Lord fight the battle. Their only weapons were their voices, lifted in song: "When [Jehoshaphat] had consulted with the people, he appointed those who should sing to the Lord, and who should praise the beauty of holiness, as they went out before the army and were saying: 'Praise the Lord, for His mercy endures forever.' Now when they began to sing and to praise, the Lord set ambushes against the people of Ammon, Moab, and Mount Seir, who had come against Judah; and they were defeated" (2 Chronicles 20:21–22).

When they began to sing, the Lord began to act. When my wife, Katrina, and I read this one night at bedtime, we immediately dropped to our knees and starting singing an old hymn of praise. And we've tried to keep singing ever since. The Devil has no weapon that can counteract the songs and praises of God's people. He can't stand the joyful music of the saints.

Truth 9: God Enriches Us Through the Experience

This story ends with God destroying the enemy while the Israelites claim a vast amount of booty: "When Jehoshaphat and his people came to take away their spoil, they found among them an abundance of valuables on the dead bodies, and precious jewelry, which they stripped off for themselves, more than they could carry away; and they were three days gathering the spoil because there was so much" (verse 25).

The booty, however, wasn't the most enriching part of the experience. Imagine how the story would now pass down to their children and grandchildren as a part of their heritage of faith. Imagine the joy at knowing their God cared for them so marvelously. "So they came to Jerusalem, with stringed instruments and harps and trumpets, to the house of the Lord" (verse 28).

I know that good will come from all we've experienced and that the spiritual growth in all of us will be worth the stress and strain of the battle. You can know that too.

Truth 10: God Intends to Give You Long-Term, Lasting Peace

The story concludes in verse 30: "Then the realm of Jehoshaphat was quiet, for his God gave him rest all around."

Your nightmare isn't going to last forever. The same Lord who has taken you into it will lead you out. He'll turn the trial into a blessing and teach you how to displace panic with peace, even as He has promised in Isaiah 26:3–4:

> You will keep him in perfect peace,
> Whose mind is stayed on You,
> Because He trusts in You.

> *Trust in the Lord forever,*
> *For in Yah, the Lord, is everlasting strength.*

The apostle Paul said that God gave us the great Old Testament stories for our instruction. Parents of prodigals are in a war for their children's souls. It's a terrible fight, but God has given us 2 Chronicles 20 to show us how to wage a victorious spiritual battle.

108

A Final Word

As we part today, remember that the prayers you've made for your child and others have been heard by our faithful God. Consider these words to you from the psalmist:

Do not fret. . . .
Trust!
Feed on His faithfulness!
Delight yourself in the Lord, and He shall give you the desires of your heart.
Commit your child to the Lord, trust also in Him, and He shall bring it to pass.
Rest in the Lord and wait patiently.
I have never seen the righteous forsaken . . . and his descendants are blessed.
Do not fret—it only causes harm.

(Adapted from Psalm 37.)

Acknowledgments

Thank you, Victoria, Hannah, and Grace, for letting me share freely a father's heart on these pages. I'm everlastingly proud of each of you—more than I can ever express—and endlessly grateful for your love and support. And of course I'm thankful to you too, Katrina, the anchor of our home and the love of my life.

I appreciate Greg Johnson, who first encouraged me to turn a personal scrapbook into a publishable manuscript, and Sealy Yates, my agent, who navigates the paper airplanes of my written pages like the skilled veteran he is.

I also want to applaud the great people at Howard Books—Jonathan Merkh, Philis Boultinghouse, Amanda Demastus, and the rest of the team.

I can't say enough about Joshua Rowe and his team at Clearly Media, who handle my media needs, online presence, and in-house marketing.

I owe a tremendous debt of thanks to all who have prayed for my family over the years, and especially to our very special church, The Donelson Fellowship in Nashville, that has supported their pastor and his family with love and prayer through thick and thin.

You're the best!

Notes

Preface

1. McDill, S. Rutherford, Jr. *Parenting the Prodigal* (Scottsdale, PA: Herald Press, 1996), p. 14.

1: The Power of Praying a Phrase of Scripture

2. Morgan, Rob. "Prayer-A-Phrase," *ParentLife*, January 1998, pp. 26–27.

3: What God Can Do

3. Morgan, Rob. *From This Verse* (Nashville, TN: Nelson, 1998), entry for April 18.

4: *The Kneeling Christian*

4. An Unknown Christian. *The Kneeling Christian* (Grand Rapids, MI: Zondervan, undated), pp. 17–18.

Notes

6: Thomas Watson on Prayer

    5. Watson, Thomas. *Gleaning from Thomas Watson* (London: Central Bible Truth Depot, 1915), p. 83.

8: John "Praying" Hyde's Remarkable Verses

    6. Moody, D. L. *Prevailing Prayer* (Chicago, IL: Moody Press, undated), p. 98.

10: Prevailing Prayer

    7. An Unknown Christian. *The Kneeling Christian* (Grand Rapids, MI: Zondervan, 1986), p. 5.

13: A Shaft of Light on a Dismal Day

    8. My heartfelt thanks to Dr. Bob Hill and his son, Rob, for their permission to include their personal information and identifying details here along with the story of Rob's personal struggles and walk with Christ.

17: Leave Room for God

    9. Thompson, Cameron V. *Master Secrets of Prayer* (Lincoln, NB: Good News Broadcasting Association, 1959), p. 51.

32: Chefoo

    10. Adapted from David Michell, *A Boy's War* (Singapore: Overseas Missionary Fellowship, 1988), pp. 138–142, with quotes from an article by Alice Hayes Taylor, "He Will Not Forsake My Children," in *Guideposts Magazine*, 1983. For more information, see www .omf.org

37: A Prayer from Augustine's *Confessions*

11. Augustine, *Confessions* (Nashville, TN: Nelson, 1999), p. 156.

38: Answers Beyond Death

12. My heartfelt thanks to Pam Frye and her siblings for their permission to include their personal information and identifying details here along with the account of their personal struggles and walk with Christ.

13. Bounds, E. M. *The Complete Works of E. M. Bounds on Prayer* (Grand Rapids, MI: Baker, 1990), p. 299.

14. Morgan, Rob. *On This Day* (Nashville, TN: Nelson, 1997), entry for May 17.

47: Blessings from Burdens

15. Adapted from Rob Morgan, "Preaching to Others When Our Own World Is Hurting," *The Preacher's Sourcebook: 2003* (Nashville, TN: Nelson, 2002), p. 50.

51: Advice from a Psychologist

16. McDill, S. Rutherford, Jr. *Parenting the Prodigal* (Scottsdale, PA: Herald Press, 1996), pp. 108–109,103,112.

58: A Potpourri of Help

17. Packer, J. I. *Knowing God* (Downers Grove, IL: InterVarsity Press, 1973), p. 219.

64: Reveal to Him

18. Adapted from a prayer composed by Alan Redpath, *Getting to Know the Will of God* (Chicago, IL: InterVarsity, 1954), p. 22.

19. Bisset, Tom. *Good News About Prodigals* (Grand Rapids, MI: Discovery House, 1997), p. 9.

66: The Healing Power of Answered Prayer

20. My heartfelt thanks to Henry Kastell and his sister, Diana, for their permission to include their personal information and identifying details here along with the account of Diana's personal struggles and walk with Christ.

67: How Can We Keep Going?

21. Adapted from Rob Morgan, "Preaching to Others When Our Own World Is Hurting," *The Preacher's Sourcebook: 2003* (Nashville, TN: Nelson, 2002), pp. 50–54.

70: Words Badly Needed

22. Meier, Paul D. *Christian Child-Rearing and Personality Development* (Grand Rapids, MI: Baker, 1977), p. ix.

23. Meier, p. 196.

77: He's Able

24. Graham, Ruth Bell. *Prodigals and Those Who Love Them* (Grand Rapids, MI: Baker, 1999), p. 87.

25. Guido, Michael. *The Michael Guido Story* (Metter, GA: The Guido Evangelistic Association, 1999), p. 123.

79: A Father's Prayer

26. My heartfelt thanks to Steve Elkins and his sons for their permission to include their personal information and identifying details here along with the prayer for his sons' personal struggles and walk with Christ.

82: A Strategic Attitude

27. Graham, Billy. *Just As I Am* (San Francisco, CA: HarperSanFrancisco/Zondervan, 1997), pp. 711, 108.

28. McDill, S. Rutherford, Jr. *Parenting the Prodigal* (Scottdale, PA: Herald Press, 1996), pp. 41–42.

92: Fasting

29. Sanders, J. Oswald. *World Prayer* (Littleton, CO: Overseas Missionary Fellowship, 1999), p. 12.

96: Dispersing Poisonous Gas

30. Taylor, Geraldine. *Behind the Ranges* (Singapore: Overseas Missionary Fellowship, 1998), p. 269.

98: The Omnipotence of Prayer

31. An Unknown Christian. *The Kneeling Christian* (Grand Rapids, MI: Zondervan, undated), p. 15

105: Praying with Hymns

32. Adapted from anonymous hymn "Come, Thou Almighty King" (c. 1757).

33. Adapted from Ray Palmer, "My Faith Looks Up to Thee" (1830).

About the Author

ROB MORGAN is the pastor of The Donelson Fellowship in Nashville, Tennessee, where he has served for more than thirty-three years. He has authored more than twenty-five books, including *The Red Sea Rules, Then Sings My Soul, From This Verse, On This Day,* and *The International Children's Devotional Bible* (all Thomas Nelson), as well as more than one hundred articles in leading Christian magazines. He conducts Bible conferences, parenting and marriage retreats, and leadership development seminars across the country. He and his wife, Katrina, live in Nashville.

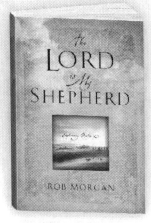
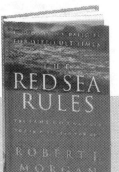

Printed in the United States
By Bookmasters